20 LESSONS

═ THAT ═

BUILD A MAN'S

FAMILY

A CONVERSATIONAL MENTORING GUIDE

"Vince Miller is a man whose life, speaking, and leadership development ministry is centered on the gospel of Jesus Christ. The fruit of Vince's life and ministry produces leaders who are personally challenged toward maturity in Christ and are able to train and equip others to spiritual maturity through developing a dependence on God and practical knowledge and application of His Word. Vince's insight into the Bible and how he challenges you to apply the gospel to how you live and lead will help you build your family on the solid foundation of Jesus Christ."

John Dickerman
Men's Leader

"Vince Miller is a game-changer! He has struck the perfect balance of relevant content, timeless wisdom, and effective methodology. There are no games or gimmicks, just bold truth and a compelling invitation to go all in!"

Tyler Van Eps
Mentor and Men's Leader

"Vince understands that defining manhood is no simple task and that every culture from the beginning of time has their own set of standards. God's plan A for building better men is for them to actively engage in the lives of other men. We see it consistently throughout the Bible. Men learn how to be men from other men — period. I never understood this until I met Vince. It's because of his dedication and passion for building better husbands, fathers, brothers, sons, leaders, and men of God that I am a better man."

Erin Hauber
Men's Leader

"Men's reactions to Vince's message consistently reveal that deep down, most desire to be men of character but don't always know how or have the courage to do so. Vince's ministry provides potent messages and tools that can and have changed men, giving them the ability to carry out lives of leadership with a focus on God. Vince's raw and emotional testimony, along with his deep-rooted desire to mentor, reshapes and restores men spiritually — which, in turn, benefits countless family members and loved ones."

Eric Bryhn
Men's Leader

"I participated in a small discipleship cohort, led by Vince, that met weekly for two years. The materials were created by Vince with God's Word at the foundation of every teaching. This experience transformed my walk with the Lord. God has gifted Vince with the extraordinary gifts of speaking and authoring material that provides men insight into God's Word, the relation to everyday life, and practical coaching to integrate into your daily walk. God has placed a high calling on men to lead their family. Will you join in the fight?"

David Ousdigian
Men's Leader

"Because of Vince Miller, I am living a lifestyle of mentoring men in Jesus Christ. He not only challenged me to this lifestyle but eliminated all my convenient excuses. I will forever gobble up any book or resource that Vince offers to improve what has become the core mission of my life. You should too."

Mike Graham
Pastor

"Vince Miller's uncomplicated approach to mentorship provides every man the opportunity to engage in the Great Commission with confidence. His ability to simplify a plan for faith, family, friends, fitness, and finances builds better men and changes a culture one man a time. This guide is a proven tool for all men pursuing a one-to-one or micro group mentorship."

Garret N Barbush
CEO Men of Iron

20 LESSONS

=== THAT ===

BUILD A MAN'S

FAMILY

A CONVERSATIONAL MENTORING GUIDE

VINCE MILLER

EQUIP PRESS

Colorado Springs

20 LESSONS THAT BUILD A MAN'S
FAMILY

A conversational
mentoring guide

First Edition: 2019
TWENTY LESSONS THAT BUILD A MAN'S FAMILY / Vince Miller
Paperback ISBN: 978-1-946453-81-5
eBook ISBN: 978-1-946453-82-2

EQUIP PRESS

Colorado Springs

TO: Mike Jacobson

FROM: _[signature]_

NOTE:

Let's build better
men for the Kingdom.

A NOTE FROM THE AUTHOR

Leading your family will test you to the core. Some days it will make you, and other days it will break you. This is because leadership completely reshapes us. Some of the lessons you will discover in this book were passed on to me by numerous leaders over many years, but I had to learn the rest from my greatest mentor—failure.

My hope for you is that these lessons give you something to discuss with a friend, relative, coworker, or even your children. I hope they will stir a discussion that will give you an opportunity to proactively pass on wisdom. May this mentoring relationship lead to greater success as you lead your business, team, non-profit, church, or your very own family.

Join a mentorship movement, and mentor or be mentored.

Keep moving forward,

USING 20 LESSONS THAT BUILD A MAN'S FAMILY

THE PURPOSE

This 20-lesson guide is for mentors to use in private reflection or conversations with others. It's written to invite leadership and character development conversations for men of any age and can be used repeatedly.

THE PROCESS

FIRST, BUILD YOURSELF

Read through one lesson each time and privately ponder the reflection questions within the lesson. Each lesson uses the B.U.I.L.D. process.

- **BEGIN** with the goal.
- **UNPACK** your thoughts.
- **INFORM** through the Bible.
- **LAND** on action steps.
- **DO** one action for one week.

SECOND, PARTNER UP

Take each lesson further by partnering up with someone else. Use the 20 lessons as a mentoring tool that takes all the guesswork out of a mentoring conversation. Partner up with a friend, relative, co-worker, or someone in your family.

THE PAYOFF

If you stay with the process for all 20 lessons, you will grow in character as a man, father, husband, and leader. Often, we just need a plan to get moving. This book provides that plan—a method and a process that results in outcomes with a rich payoff.

ABOUT VINCE MILLER

Abandoned by his drug-using father at the age of two, Vince Miller grew up in a challenging and anxiety-producing environment. He endured the strain of his mother's two failed marriages as well as her poor choices and drug use. Fortunately, during Vince's formative teen years, his grandfather, a man of faith, stepped up to mentor Vince, guiding him through a particularly difficult period.

Though he resisted initially, Vince became a follower of Christ at the age of twenty. Soon after, he would be with his grandfather on his deathbed as cancer took his life. At that time, Vince committed before God to give back by mentoring men as his grandfather had mentored him. Vince's story demonstrates the importance of mentors who support others in overcoming the enormous hurdles that manhood, mentoring, fatherhood, and leadership present to a man who wants to live in faith and character.

Audiences respond to Vince's stories and teaching that motivate, convict, and sometimes even shock. He inspires men to lead and mentor others with an intelligent argument for faith and stories of choices he made as a man, husband, father, and leader.

After serving in notable organizations for over twenty-six years (including Young Life, InterVarsity, and TCU Football), Vince founded Resolute, a non-profit organization focused on providing men with tools for mentorship. He's written sixteen books and Bible study handbooks and produced small group videos that serve as resources for mentorship. He also wrote *The Men's Daily Devotional*, which is read by thousands daily.

If you are looking for a motivational and engaging communicator for your next retreat, conference, or event, reach out to Vince Miller directly through his website: www.vincemiller.com

TABLE OF CONTENTS

THE PURPOSE OF MARRIAGE

"Many people spend more time in planning the wedding than they do in planning the marriage."

—Zig Ziglar

"'And the two shall become one flesh.' So they are no longer two but one flesh."

—Mark 10:8

A PURPOSE FOR MARRIAGE

God has a purpose for marriage that is very different than what we initially realize. Marriage is His tool for producing a change in the life of two people. He uses marriage to reshape the rough edges in our character. He uses marriage to reorient our selfishness. He uses marriage to reform our spiritual perspectives. Through the relationship of marriage, we will be reshaped, reoriented, and reformed with the intention of making us into better men—the men He wants us to be.

THREE CHANGES WE DISCOVER IN MARRIAGE
CHANGE ONE | CHARACTER RESHAPED

One challenge that many do not expect to encounter in marriage is the fact that we can no longer hide our weaknesses and insecurities. Your wife will get to know you in a way that surpasses even your parents' knowledge. She's going to eventually be able to discern when you're lying, hurt, broken, confused, absent, and unfulfilled. While you used to be able to conceal these matters from the general public, your spouse will notice them and might even point them out—maybe unfairly. And while you will not meet her insight with enthusiasm, it's one way marriage changes you. For when the truth about yourself is exposed, you have the potential for change if you're receptive. The longer you're married, the more you will realize this is true. Increasingly, your wife will know you— and you her—and your character will be more visible, examined, and exposed. And if she loves God and His Word, then hopefully she will guide you toward becoming the man God wants you to be. And this relationship and process proves and shapes our character.

CHANGE TWO | SELFISHNESS REORIENTED

All people are inherently selfish and self-centered. And if you happen to be single, you can do what you want. It is pretty easy. You don't have anybody to check-in with, report to, or attempt to work things out with—except possibly a boss or roommate, though you can choose to opt out of these relationships. But after that first day of marriage, everything changes. You move from one place into another, and someone else moves in too—permanently. It requires a whole new frame of mind, which many don't understand. It's a move from one to "oneness," where two people "become one in the flesh." And part of this is God's plan for us to become less of "me" and more of "we." Many of us, however, move in with the same old selfish expectations, thinking marriage is just going to be life as usual, but with a roommate and some sexual privileges. How wrong we are. Brave unions address our selfishness and its festering wounds, inadequate ideas, poor practices, and acute attitudes that prevent oneness.

CHANGE THREE | SPIRITUALLY REFORMED

In marriage, we discover something special. While to many it seems to be only a physical union joined by a contract, it's primarily a spiritual union joined by an eternal commitment. Marriage is not exclusively about reshaping our character or reorienting our selfishness, but a spiritual covenant that we make to God and commit to for a lifetime. It reforms us at the deepest level. What God joins together is something no man can separate. Like two colors of sand poured into a single container, when one man and one woman join together, something spiritual occurs that makes the two inseparable. We typically understand this binding when a marriage goes through challenges that endanger the connection. And marriage will have its share of challenges.

When things go awry and the enemy attacks, eventually you will discover that you cannot do marriage without God. These challenges will prove how hard it is for you to change, and how impossible it is to change your spouse. Let these moments drive you to submission, letting God change you. After all, God never changes. When your marriage bumps into Him, you are hopefully smart enough to give in to Him. Because marriage is God's institution, it is always under attack; your response should be spiritual attentiveness to a spiritual reformation of the mind, will, and action.

REFLECTION & MENTORSHIP

BEGIN

- Marriage is God's tool for producing a change in the life of two people.

UNPACK

- What excites you about marriage, and what challenges you about marriage?
- What one principle have you learned about marriage that has changed your perspective on its purpose in your life?

INFORM

- What image comes to mind when you hear the term "one flesh?"
- Which of the three points above on marriage strike you as the most challenging?

LAND

- What issues do you need to address in your marriage?
- What steps do you need to take to see God's purposes differently?

DO

- Identify one change you will make in your marriage.
- Submit yourself to that change.
- Invite a friend or mentor into accountability with you on this topic.

ROMANTICIZING MARRIAGE

"Married men live longer than single men. But married men are a lot more willing to die."

—Johnny Carson

"And the two shall become one flesh. So they are no longer two but one flesh. What therefore God has joined together, let not man separate."

—Mark 10:8–9

CRUSHED EXPECTATIONS

It can be a real emotional letdown when you're sitting in a counseling session with your spouse and realize that you or your spouse's expectations are not being met. This might be the first moment of the realization that your thoughts and expectations about your marriage were very different.

Many men testify to encountering a moment when their wife exclaims, "You're not the man I thought I married." Or maybe you will say or think the same about your wife. This can be an awkward moment. Many couples are surprised by this moment because they experienced early in their relationship what they believed to be a deep love. Only now do they discover it might have been love built on emotion or feeling that led them to over-romanticize their marriage. But marriage is deeper than mere infatuation.

THREE PRINCIPLES TO REMEMBER ABOUT MARRIAGE
ONE | COUPLES ENCOUNTER STRUGGLE

If you talk to couples who have been married for fifty years or more, you will discover that they often confess to multiple years of conflict with each other. This is shocking for many. It was for me. But marriage is not always as pretty, perfect, and romantic as we want it to be. It's full of ups and downs. It is going to include struggles with health, finances, children, and each other.

Many couples who have been married for fifty years or more will tell you that there was often a prolonged length of time (sometimes five to ten years) that was challenging for both of them. Even if they're currently very happily married, they may tell you about a severe and substantial season when they weren't sure they were going to make it—an event or conflict had put their marriage in danger. This often surprises us because we romanticize marriage in a way that we should not.

It's fine to want a romantic marriage or the very best marriage, but we shouldn't imagine that the experience will only be great. This is never true in any relationship. And while some think they are going to have perfect sexual intimacy all the time, and others think they are going to have complete emotional intimacy all the time, our dreams are quickly crushed when we discover each other's failings, faults, and shortcomings. Remember, struggle is inevitable; you are either in one, coming out of one, or about to head into it. Anticipate it.

TWO | MARRIAGE IS A COMMITMENT

As we enter marriage, we usually don't realize that our commitment to marriage is more important than the contract of marriage. Contracts are made to be broken; ask any attorney. When push comes to shove, we will look for a way out of a contract. It's in our human nature. We love to justify, to look for excuses, and when we feel pain, we run for safety. Commitment eludes half of all Christian marriages today. At the start of a marriage, few couples imagine they could ever end up divorced, but 50% of all Christian marriages do end in divorce. This fact remains unchanged.

The remedy is a single word: commitment. Older couples will resoundingly affirm that commitment was the one thing that got them through the hardest moments in their marriage. Commitment, not a contract, with both members engaged. That's all it takes—commitment, commitment, and more commitment. I have seen many marriages face challenges, and some of them are ugly. And yet, as ugly as they are, the beauty of commitment is far more significant. Just keep this verse in mind: "What therefore God has joined together, let not man separate" (Mark 10:9).

THREE | SHARE WHAT YOU WANT AND NEED

When we romanticize marriage, we, by nature, begin to look elsewhere when our unspoken needs are not being met. Maybe it starts by looking at other couples and seeing their relationship only through the eyes of perfection. And then our discontent escalates as we seek out the physical or emotional attention we want, or maybe need, from another person who is not our spouse. Before we know it, we are emotionally or physically involved with another person. And why? Maybe because we never verbalized our wants and needs.

This escalation of romanticizing always lends to tragic results. It attempts to undermine the joy of relationship, and it has long-lasting negative ramifications. The way we combat this destructive path is not only by checking our self-centeredness but by actively sharing our wants and needs. Many couples forgo these conversations for too long, which creates an emotional and physical disconnection that becomes increasingly difficult to mend. An anthill of need turns into molehills of latent needs that go unmet first for weeks, then months, and then years. In this void of conversation, we leave a vacuum of unspoken need on the table that often leads to harbored feelings that must be expressed and responded to. For the sake of your marriage, your relationships, your future, your children, and your faith—have the conversation. Speak up and let your heart be known. Stop the silence. It might lead to something beautiful.

REFLECTION & MENTORSHIP
BEGIN

- Marriage is not always as romantic as we think it will be. It should be more than romantic; it should be a strong, loving commitment to open communication between two people.

UNPACK

- What are your aspirations for your current or future marriage?
- Do you think your aspirations are realistic?
- What do you think your spouse wants more or less of in your marriage?

INFORM

- Mark 10:8–9 notes the "one-flesh" relationship in marriage. What types of things challenge "one-fleshiness" in marriages today?
- Which of the three principles captured your attention today?

LAND

- What challenges do you face as you pursue honest and open communication in your marriage?
- What steps do you need to take overcome these challenges?

DO

- Take one action that demonstrates your commitment to your wife.
- Invite accountability that commits to following through.

EMOTIONAL GROWTH IN MARRIAGE

"As for my secret to staying married, my wife tells me that if I ever decide to leave, she is coming with me."

—Jon Bon Jovi

"Therefore a man shall leave his father and his mother and hold fast to his wife, and they shall become one flesh."

—Genesis 2:24

MARRIAGE IS EMOTIONALLY CHALLENGING

Marriage can be a great blessing and a great challenge all at the same time. Problems often arise because we men do not invest the time we should in an emotional connection with our wives. But for most women, and I would suggest men too, the emotional connection is an essential item in the relationship. As men, we can be clueless that we are reaching an emotional deficit with our wives, which usually results in an increase in stress and conflict. Often this occurs in the form of reactions and responses that seem to arise "suddenly." And the awful part of the experience for men is that these complications continue for days or seasons in our relationship. While they catch us by surprise, they should not.

FIVE WAYS TO GROW EMOTIONALLY IN MARRIAGE

ONE | NAME THE EMOTIONAL RESPONSES YOU'RE HAVING TOWARD YOUR SPOUSE

Emotional responses by either party are often about important things. Men often wonder, "Why is she so worked up?" And herein lies the issue. Emotional reactions are symptoms of a greater issue that should signal that something in your marriage is off-balance and needs attention. So if your emotional response is anger, disappointment, sadness, or disgust, just name what you are feeling, but try not to do this in an attacking manner.

TWO | IDENTIFY THE EMOTION AND LABEL IT

This is a critical step because it teaches you to slow down—to not just react but to identify the feeling you're having and look at it with a little perspective. In other words, you need to see it outside of yourself. Robert Plutchik, who has studied emotions, suggests that there are eight basic emotions you should be able to identify and name:

1. **Fear**
2. **Anger**
3. **Sadness**
4. **Joy**
5. **Disgust**
6. **Surprise**
7. **Trust**
8. **Anticipation**

In this case, we are talking about negative emotions: fear, anger, sadness, or disgust. Can you name that emotion you are experiencing or that you see in your spouse?

THREE | REFLECT ON HOW YOU HAVE EXPERIENCED THIS IN THE PAST

Often, when you have an emotional reaction, it is because you have experienced a similar event in the past. So, for instance, you may have "messages" or "tapes" in your head from painful or negative childhood experiences. If you hear something from your spouse that resembles those past painful tapes, you are likely to respond emotionally regardless (and this is important) of whether it was meant that way or not. When your emotions are triggered (I call this "emotional hijacking"), it is time to deal with your issues, not the problems of your spouse. You should reflect on what that issue is. Be more concerned about naming yours than pointing out hers.

FOUR | TRY TO SHORTEN THE TIME OF THE REACTION/EMOTION

Negative emotions tend to hang around for a while. After identifying the emotion and understanding where it came from, work on shortening the time that the reaction or emotion affects your relationship with your spouse. If the normal time is two days of relational stress, work on resolving it in one day; if within a few hours, then within an hour. The sooner you can normalize your reaction, the sooner the relationship can reestablish its healthy rhythm.

FIVE | INVITE YOUR SPOUSE TO HELP YOU PROCESS THE EMOTIONS

Often when your emotions are hijacked, your spouse is left wondering what in the world happened. It helps to explain to her what is going on with you and what you are trying to figure out. And be honest about what you believe triggered your reaction—not as a matter of blame, but to increase her awareness of your sensitivity to the issue. Tell her also that you are working on "moving through it" more quickly, so she knows you are aware and working to avoid the emotional hijacking.

REFLECTION & MENTORSHIP

BEGIN

- The emotional connection is an essential item in a marriage. It's one we often ignore, and we must get smarter at understanding, communicating, and sharing our emotions.

UNPACK

- Describe the emotional relationship between your mother and father. What was healthy? What was unhealthy?
- What do you think you have inadvertently picked up from them?

- How would you describe your wife's family of origin?
- What do you think she has picked up from them?

INFORM

- What does it mean to become one flesh?
- How does a lack of emotional connection prohibit oneness?
- After reading the five points above, what captures your attention?

LAND

- What challenges do you face as you grow emotionally in your marriage? Why?
- What steps do you need to take to overcome these challenges?

DO

- Identify what you need to share emotionally with your wife this week.
- When and how do you plan to do that?
- Invite positive accountability to take this action and report back on what happened.

NURTURING YOUR MARRIAGE

"By all means, marry. If you get a good wife, you'll become happy; if you get a bad one, you'll become a philosopher."

—Socrates

"Therefore encourage one another and build one another up, just as you are doing."

—1 Thessalonians 5:11

NURTURE IS ESSENTIAL TO LIFE

Often, we don't think of nurturing as a masculine activity, but it's extremely masculine. And there's a lot of leadership, care, and development involved. Nurture is the process of caring for the development of another, which is primary to our role as a leader, husband, and father.

Think of caring for your marriage like nurturing a plant. Yeah, I know, some people are not that great at cultivating plants and frequently kill them. Others have what we call "green thumbs" because they are great at caring for plants and fostering growth. And the difference between these two types of people is how they nurture the plants under their care. In the same way, a neglected marriage is one that, well, fails. It's one where two people drift apart, harbor resentment, leave issues unaddressed, and give license to sin. Many married men will attest to a season where they've felt like their marriages were unnurtured, as will many women. Perhaps we're pursuing careers, kids, and tons of activities—but we're not nurturing. We're bowing to the idols of involvement, achievement, and personal success; we've forgotten to nurture our relationship with God and our relationship with our spouse.

THINGS TO KEEP IN MIND TO SUCCESSFULLY NURTURE
ONE | NURTURE IS A MINDSET

So many of us have gone about seeking a wife, winning her over, and putting on a display of love. Then comes the wedding, and we think we have arrived. We are led to believe that we've accomplished what we came to do—we've found the woman of our dreams, and we've married her. When we have the mentality that we're done, what we believe we have is a trophy wife. But your wife is not a trophy to be possessed, gained, or earned—she's the image of God now one with you. A trophy mentality is deadly to ongoing nurturing activities in marriage. When you get married, you have only just begun the work of nurture. It's as if you've just seeded a new plant. Your marriage is a living relationship that must be cared for in a way that's either going to make it grow or die.

TWO | NURTURE IS A REGULAR CONVERSATION

We take for granted the nurturing need for regular face-to-face communication. And this is not exchanging facts about our day, or opinions about the latest political happening—we're talking about meaningful sharing that is more transparent than a casual exchange. Notice the patterns in your day. With urgency, you come home at the end of the day only hoping to get through the evening without a major catastrophe. Or by the time evening comes, you are too exhausted to engage in a meaningful dialogue, as it requires more energy than you care to give. Too many successive days like this, and this pattern will become the norm and your marriage will lack the appropriate level of nurture. Neither you nor your spouse will receive the nourishment you need.

A meaningful conversation about your feelings regarding the present and future is a basic nurturing need. It's like water, sun, and fertilizer for a dying plant. And remember, you can't just flood a plant with water, sun, and fertilizer—it needs a steady drip. You should be scheduling time for intentional engagement. If your home does not provide a conducive environment, go ahead and plan an occasional getaway at a bed-n-breakfast or a dinner out at a nice restaurant. You should be leading here and not waiting for your wife to prompt you. Plan it for her. And don't do it selfishly; do it to nurture her and yourself.

THREE | NURTURE INVOLVES LEARNING FROM OTHERS

We need other people in marital relationships to speak into our lives at various stages to challenge us emotionally, mentally, physically, and spiritually. Over your marriage journey, you need to find compatible couples with whom you can spend time—including some who are further along in life than you. You should feel comfortable asking them questions and engaging in dialogue about married life. Look for couples who will be transparent with you about life, relationships, and the future. You might find these people at church or in your family. Marriage retreats or seminars can offer great opportunities to get to know compatible couples and begin forging these relationships. Nothing is more helpful than learning from others.

REFLECTION & MENTORSHIP

BEGIN

- Marriage must be nurtured like any living organism; a nurturing mindset, nurturing conversation, and insight from other relationships will help sustain growth and vitality.

UNPACK

- What do you currently do to nurture your marriage?
- What would you like to do to nurture your marriage?
- What do you think your spouse needs in order to feel nurtured in your marriage?

INFORM

- 1 Thessalonians 5:11 references the need for encouragement. How would you rate current levels of encouragement in your marriage on a scale of 1–10? Why?
- What would move this up a notch?
- What convicts you about the topic of nurture?

LAND

- What challenges do you face in becoming a more nurturing husband and father?
- What steps do you need to take to overcome these challenges?

DO

- Do one thoughtful, planned, nurturing activity this week for your wife.
- Plan to report back to your mentor or discussion partner on how this went.

CONFLICT ON THE HOME FRONT

"Peace is not absence of conflict; it is the ability to handle conflict by peaceful means."

—*Ronald Reagan*

"Hatred stirs up conflict, but love covers all offenses."

—*Proverbs 10:12*

IT'S GOING TO HAPPEN

In families and marriage, conflict is inevitable. It will happen. And in some seasons, it will feel like conflict is the only thing you manage. You might be facing a struggle over finances, a dispute over parenting strategies, or a challenge because of your sin. Since conflict is unavoidable, those who anticipate, lead, and successfully manage these moments have a distinct advantage. The next time you encounter conflict, acknowledge these five laws.

FIVE LAWS FOR MANAGING CONFLICT IN YOUR HOME

LAW ONE | MANAGE YOUR ANXIETY

Conflict is not always a bad thing, but we can become quickly bothered by it. This is part of the reason for increased levels of marital and family stress. We need to keep in mind that conflict is normal. Frequently, it invites clarity where there is confusion and resolves a silent tension that needs to be made known. Many marriages and families are conflict-averse because they think conflict is a reflection on their deficiencies. But it isn't your responsibility to prevent the arrival of conflict; how you lead through the conflict is the variable you can control. If as a husband or a father you can determine the root issues underlying the conflict without getting hooked by emotional insecurities, you will be able to lead more successfully in the midst of these encounters. Don't let yourself get baited and hooked. It's hard to help your wife and children from a state of anxiety; remember that they will naturally respond in kind to your emotional cues.

LAW TWO | LISTEN AND CLARIFY

When emotions get elevated, family members tend to stop listening to each other because their capacity to listen is being hijacked by the emotional need to be heard. You can deescalate a conflict by sitting down and listening—with precision—and clarifying or repeating what's being said. Most of the time in a conflict, people want to be both heard and understood. In the process of listening, you are helping them to gain a voice and a hearing they feel they don't have; in the process, you get a better understanding of what's happening. By listening, you give others the time to ramp down emotionally.

LAW THREE | IDENTIFY DESIRED OUTCOMES

As we listen, we should be on a quest to identify the outcomes desired. Sometimes, when we are in conflict with each other, we don't realize that the other party may have similar or even common goals, and we are just arguing over the best way to get there. If you know the result your family member wants, then you can help them figure out how they can achieve their goal—and achieve it together. But remember, though we tend to focus on the outcomes, just as important are the lessons learned through conflict and the relational wins we enjoy on the other side of the conflict.

LAW FOUR | STATE NEXT STEPS (IF THERE ARE ANY)

Is your next step another discussion? Is it a change in how you and your wife handle finances? Is it a search for a new way of parenting? Is it a new discipline that needs to be built? Whatever it is, identify it and ensure that family members are clear on what they need to do and when they need to do it. Build in some accountability to ensure that promises are kept and decisions are followed through, thereby avoiding another eruption. These steps will demonstrate to everyone that you have listened and want to reconcile future issues. In addition, you will have equipped others to manage conflicts better themselves.

LAW FIVE | INCLUDE OUTSIDE COUNSEL AS NEEDED

Sometimes you'll hit an obstacle as you try to resolve an issue with your spouse or family. Outside counsel can help two or more disgruntled members to work toward a solution. You'll need to find a neutral party, respected by both parties, to fill this role. Licensed marriage and family counselors are a great example. Remember, there is nothing wrong with seeing a therapist, as they can often mediate an issue where the participants are too emotionally tangled. Every marriage or family at some point is going to need to seek outside help to gain perspective. Asking someone to help mediate and resolve a matter with biblical insight is a humbling yet wise choice. Don't be afraid to ask others for help when you get stuck; it's better than hiding the issue or attempting to handle it on your own.

Emotions and insecurities can prevent families from working through issues that are usually simple to solve. If you as a husband and father can help lower the emotional intensity of everyone involved and help them look objectively at the situation from the perspective of the desired outcome, solutions are often easy to find. Conflict is a healthy test to see if you can embrace it as such.

REFLECTION & MENTORSHIP
BEGIN
- Conflict is inevitable in families; therefore, those who anticipate, lead, and personally manage these moments will have a distinct advantage.

UNPACK
- What kinds of conflict are you equipped to manage? What kinds are more challenging for you?
- Does a certain type of personality make you particularly anxious in times of conflict? Why is this so?

INFORM
- Why do we forget to handle conflict in a peaceful way?
- The proverb above says love is powerful for conflict resolution. What does love have to do with conflict?

- Of the five laws above, which could you better follow in your family and marriage? Share why and be transparent.

LAND

- What is one issue you need to address in how you handle conflict?
- What steps do you need to take?

DO

- Commit to embracing one law above this week.
- When and how will you plan to accomplish this?

LOVE AND RESPECT

"It's more than a feeling..."

—*Boston*

"However, let each one of you love his wife as himself, and let the wife see that she respects her husband."

—*Ephesians 5:33*

WE BOTH NEED SOMETHING

It should not come as a surprise that men and women are wired differently and thus have differing needs. While we all need love and respect, men and women each distinctively need more of one than the other. Women by nature want to know that their husbands love and adore them. Men by nature desire to know that their wives respect and honor them. And while we each need to give and receive both love and respect, expressing love is an essential focus for a husband, and demonstrating respect is a necessary focus for a wife. Failing to understand the importance of these essentials can leave a marriage wanting for more. When both partners even attempt to meet these needs, the marriage has an opportunity to flourish.

THERE IS SOMETHING FOR BOTH OF US

HUSBANDS: ACTIVE LOVE IS YOUR ESSENTIAL

The operative word is "active" love. Love is always active and must be expressed in tangible ways to your wife. Love should not be assumed or merely mentioned but demonstrated actively. It's something you communicate in variety for your wife.

The apostle Paul describes love most brilliantly in 1 Corinthians 13:5–7. "Love is patient and kind; love does not envy or boast; it is not arrogant or rude. It does not insist on its own way; it is not irritable or resentful; it does not rejoice at wrongdoing, but rejoices with the truth. Love bears all things, believes all things, hopes all things, endures all things."

You've probably skimmed those verses before, or maybe they are very familiar to you. But before you read on, go back and reread them and ask yourself how well you live out the listed characteristics of love with your wife. Don't read them with regret or shame; read them and consider the activities of love you could deploy in your marriage. It might be worth taking a few minutes to meditate on them at some point as you think about your marriage.

- **Patient** | How can I be actively patient and love my wife?
- **Kind** | How can I be actively kind and love my wife?
- **Does not envy** | How can I be actively generous and love my wife?
- **Does not boast** | How can I be actively modest and love my wife?
- **Is not arrogant** | How can I be actively humble and love my wife?
- **Is not rude** | How can I be actively polite and love my wife?
- **Does not insist your way** | How can I actively insist on her way and love my wife?
- **Is not irritable** | How can I be actively easy-going and love my wife?
- **Is not resentful** | How can I be actively satisfied and love my wife?
- **Does not rejoice in wrongdoing** | How can I actively celebrate and love my wife?
- **Rejoices in the truth** | How can I actively be truthful and love my wife?

If this list says anything, it's that love is more than a feeling (thanks Boston for getting this right). And it's not just empty verbiage. Love is active, which means that you have to do something. All these actions say "I love you" in a variety of ways to your wife.

When we become husbands, we must learn how to demonstrate love in new ways, regardless of whether we had great role models or not. Learning to love your wife in a variety of ways is essential. And loving her in a way she wants to be loved is an art. You need to love her differently than any other woman. Over time you must learn her language of love. You must give love in the way she wants to be loved, not merely the way you want to deliver it. You might even have to unlearn the way you have shown love in the past. And contrary to popular opinion, I know my wife has more than five love languages; sorry, Gary Chapman.

The last verse in the above passage from 1 Corinthians is about the enduring nature of active love. "Love bears all things, believes all things, hopes all things, endures all things." In other words, real love is not temporary or dependent on your present feeling toward your wife. It bears, believes, hopes, and endures beyond present feelings about yourself, your circumstances, or your wife. This is because love goes the distance. And an ongoing demonstration of love gives your wife confidence in your commitment, which again is a demonstration of love. It's an active love bound by commitment, not a feeling.

WIVES: RESPECT IS YOUR ESSENTIAL

Now, men, after you are done reading this, you may want to share this chapter in whole with your wife.

Hands down, more than anything, a man desires respect. It's his native language. Just as romancing, cherishing, and tenderness are the native love language of a wife, respect is the basic hunger of a husband. Deserved or not, men want it and need it, and yes, this can seem like a foreign language to our wives. Contrary to popular opinion, we don't need respect to feed our egos. And respect is not to be confused with an occasional compliment. Respect is our way of knowing that trust, confidence, and credibility are being built in our marriages, with our children, and in our leadership. And men, we may not even know how much we need it until we experience a moment that smells of disrespect, and then our need is elevated to contentious fight-or-flight heights. When our wives subtly shame us before others, when they disagree with us before our children, or make a decision independent of us that offends specific values—an alarm goes off inside us.

Mark Gungor, author of *Laugh Your Way to a Better Marriage*, makes the following observation about the male need for respect:

"So what is it that men want? In a word, men want respect. That means a man wants to be held in esteem and to be shown consideration and appreciation—even when he makes mistakes. He wants to be seen as a hero, especially in the eyes of his bride. He needs someone to believe in him when the odds are stacked against him. If a man doesn't feel respected, he's destined to act in a way reminiscent of the obnoxious, 'I-can't-get-no-respect,' Rodney Dangerfield. He becomes insulting, bug-eyed, and generally gross."

This isn't sexist, chauvinistic, bigoted, or discriminatory. It's the way a man flourishes. Men desire respect for who they are, and who they are is usually expressed in what they do. Men seek honor and respect for their hard work, their provision for their families, and their problem-solving prowess. If they don't feel respected, they feel their identity as a man is diminished or attacked. And this is a bit of a mystery to a woman, but husbands will promptly agree that respect in the home helps them to flourish in their role within the home, in outside relationships, and even in their identity. Even when you fall short as a leader, respect from the woman you love is a powerful force in your life.

What's interesting is that if a man feels that he must always earn his wife's respect, without merely possessing it as a husband, he may experience a love and respect standoff. Like women want to be loved for who they are, a man wants to be appreciated for who he is—not for the idealized version his wife might envision. We want our wives to work to catch us doing things right, and not exclusively point out all the wrong things we have done. When we get caught doing something right, we become motivated as a man and a husband.

Just as a man's love for his wife brings out the best in her, so a woman's respect for her husband brings out the best in him. In both cases, we make a choice to provide what the other needs—and it is a choice—and the result is an enduring and loving marriage. Men who withhold their active love undermine their marriage. The same is true for women who withhold their respect.

REFLECTION & MENTORSHIP
BEGIN

- Women by nature want to know that their husbands love and adore them. Men by nature desire to know that their wives respect and honor them.

UNPACK

- How did you see your father love your mother?
- How did you see your mother respect your father?

INFORM

- In Ephesians 5:33, we see a beautiful connection between love and respect. What do you think happens when one side is not delivering on his or her end of the commitment—when love is bankrupt or respect is lacking?
- What issues do you face in the love-and-respect relationship?
- What issues do you think your wife faces?

LAND

- Identify one issue you're facing in your marriage and write it down.
- Take steps to address and pray for this issue.

DO

- Invite your wife to tell you when she feels love is lacking. You could consider letting her read the section above and let her respond.
- Using your answers in the "Land" section, develop a plan of action to talk with your wife about your need for respect.
- Invite a friend or mentor to hold you accountable in having this hard conversation. Report back to your mentor or discussion partner about how the conversation went and what you learned.

SEXUAL SATISFACTION

"You know that look that women get when they want to have sex? Me neither."

—Steve Martin

"The husband should give to his wife her conjugal rights, and likewise the wife to her husband."

—1 Corinthians 7:3

YOU THINK ABOUT IT THE MOST, BUT YOU TALK ABOUT IT THE LEAST

Some conversations are hard for couples to have, and there is none more awkward for some Christian couples than having a conversation about sex. Given that we live in a culture that is saturated with sexual images and innuendos, it is ironic that many couples cannot communicate well about their sexual desires in a healthy and straight-forward manner. In many cases, the result of not being able to express our wishes and desires leads to hidden sexual frustration. We reach a standoff that can become complicated and challenging to overcome—or so we think. But why bury this conversation when sexual satisfaction may only be a discussion away?

THREE THINGS YOU CAN DO TO INCREASE SEXUAL SATISFACTION
ONE | SEXUAL SATISFACTION MATTERS

Now, this may seem obvious, but it's not verbalized in many marriages: you and your wife both want more and better sex. Yes, you both want it! And the pleasure that comes from it. But if you never talk about sex, then you may be missing a big part of what makes it satisfying. Sex is communication, which is just as important as any other form of oral or physical communication. For a woman, an *emotional connection* may be an aphrodisiac (although I believe this is a generalization). For a man, *visual or verbal stimulation* might be a powerful turn-on, (although I also think this is a generalization). In the end, regardless of what stimulates a man or a woman, I believe both want the same thing—**deeper communication and intimacy**—yet we both go about it a little differently. It's our responsibility to understand this subtlety and be courageous enough to engage in honest communication to ensure that our spouse's intimacy needs are met. Dr. Marcus Bachmann, the president of Counseling Care, a faith-based counseling practice in Minnesota, says, "Sex is about giving, not taking." We need to be better at giving, not just having. And for goodness sakes, we need to have some sexual fun.

Furthermore, when sexual satisfaction is lacking, it breeds a "communication resentment" that can lead to emotional distance, frustration, and anger. As that resentment grows, you are in danger of growing apart, which is why sexless marriages are not honoring to God. Dr. Bachmann said to me in a recent interview, "A sexless marriage is not God's idea. God created sex." While the sexual aspect of marriage may need to be discussed and negotiated so that it's enjoyable for both parties, long-term abstinence for a couple is unhealthy and a sign that we are avoiding required communication.

TWO | OVERCOME THE SHAME

Shame is one of the challenges every man must address. Shame regarding sex may result from subtle messages we embrace about sex from childhood. Or it may be an issue we have with being vulnerable enough to admit to our spouse our sexual ignorance or needs. Men don't like to be exposed, and this type of conversation is a profoundly vulnerable discussion. We are no more vulnerable than when we are naked in bed and secretly longing to have a new sexual experience. We may hesitate to broach the subject out of embarrassment, even though we know the conversation is what stimulates the change. When you are reluctant to discuss this issue with your spouse, it can become a shaming pattern that has the potential to hold you a prisoner. This is not shaming from God who created physical pleasure for marriage, but shame from the Evil One who wants to keep the two of you apart. As Dr. Bachmann told me, "Sexual messages should be exchanged early in the day, in the middle of the day, and at the end of the day—these should be celebrated." And I think we should shout yes in agreement. So maybe you need to text your wife right now.

THREE | TRY HAVING A CONVERSATION

Are you ready to start the conversation? A straightforward communication tactic can enhance any hard or challenging issue that you or your spouse face—and this tactic is regular prayer. Now that may sound way too simple, but let me explain. As Christian men, we should believe that Christ is the center of our marriages. Some things are hard to talk with our spouse about, but both of us can speak to God about those things—together. And you cannot speak to God about important issues without the two of you starting to respond to the very things you are asking God for help with. So talk with God about your need for sexual satisfaction. This is easier to do if you and your wife are already in the habit of praying together daily. In a healthy relationship, anything is fair game to talk to God about. Praying for help in your physical, sexual relationship will likely lead to conversations about it, which can lead to greater understanding between the two of you. Try it.

REFLECTION & MENTORSHIP

BEGIN

- Sex, intercourse, intimacy, making love, or whatever a married couple wants to call it is an important and natural component of marriage. It is something God created for us and wants both of you to enjoy.

UNPACK

- How often are you involved in or exposed to appropriate conversations about sex? How does this compare to the frequency of your exposure or participation in sexual joking or innuendos? Why do you think this is so?
- Do you agree or disagree that Christians have a particularly hard time talking about sex? Why?
- How was the topic of sexuality treated in your childhood home? What was your view of sex as a young adult? How does that differ from your current perspective?

INFORM

- The Bible gives a married husband and wife permission to exercise "conjugal rights." What do you think this confers?
- After reading the three points above, what captures your attention?

LAND

- What issues do you face in finding sexual satisfaction?
- What issues do you believe your wife faces in finding sexual satisfaction?
- What steps do you need to take to overcome these challenges?

DO

- Have a conversation about sex with your wife and see where it leads.

PURITY IN RELATIONSHIPS

"The proof of spiritual maturity is not how pure you are but awareness of your impurity. That very awareness opens the door to grace."

—Philip Yancey

"Flee from sexual immorality. Every other sin a person commits is outside the body, but the sexually immoral person sins against his own body."

—1 Corinthians 6:18

SEXUAL ETHICS

The topic of sexual ethics is getting a lot of press today. The #MeToo movement has been highlighting a lot of poor male behavior. But issues of this nature shouldn't surprise us given the increase and even constant bombardment of sexual themes on radio and television and the prolific presence of pornography on the web. This raises the question: In an age of sexual bombardment, how should a man of God conduct himself sexually with men and women in life?

THE PLAN FOR PURITY

ONE | GOD'S STANDARD IS NOT A HINT

Consider these words of the Apostle Paul in Ephesians 5:3–4. "But sexual immorality and all impurity or covetousness must not even be named among you, as is proper among saints. Let there be no filthiness nor foolish talk nor crude joking, which are out of place, but instead let there be thanksgiving."

The NIV translates this as "not even a hint," which is the standard for a follower of Christ. We wouldn't need a #MeToo movement if we would only follow God's #notevenahint mandate; impurity of any kind, including sexual impurity, is just not compatible with God's plan nor our holiness. Sexual expression, while permissible, has appropriate boundaries in the Bible. And while contemporary radio, television, and the web attempt to redefine these boundaries by turning sexual acts, innuendos, and joking into entertainment, this permissive attitude is not appropriate for conduct among followers of Christ.

TWO | PURITY IS THE AIM

"Not a hint" means that our relationships with women are to be pure and respectful; we should treat all women as if they were our relatives, siblings, mother, or grandmother. We should be protective of women who, like us, are made in God's image, taking care to never exploit, objectify, or act condescendingly toward anyone. As Christians, we are called to treat all people with honor and respect.

Whenever a relationship with a woman other than your spouse becomes sensitive, suggestive, sensual, or sexual in talk or touch, you should back out, regardless the cost; you are in violation of God's standard of purity. For example, when Joseph ran from the sexual advances of Potiphar's wife, she retaliated by having him thrown into prison. Joseph correctly valued his integrity, holiness, and purity above physical pleasure (or the limited personal freedom afforded to a slave).

THREE | LOCKER ROOM TALK IS NOT ACCEPTABLE

Both men and women are capable of vulgar sexual conversation with friends. You have likely heard both genders engage in hypersexual talk. Men often write it off as "locker room talk," as if there is a place where such language and conversation is acceptable. We do this because we falsely believe the lie that "men will be men." But if the standard is that our lives display "not even a hint" of sexual immorality or any impurity, this is not a conversation we should ever be a party to. We are temples of the Holy Spirit. Anywhere we go, wherever we have a discussion, God is there, and we grieve Him when that conversation is impure or immoral. Locker room talk has no place in the life of a godly man.

The next time you are in a situation where language, attitudes, or actions cross a line into impurity, remind yourself: Not even a hint.

REFLECTION & MENTORSHIP
BEGIN

- Sexual purity is an important part of your spiritual life as you navigate a world that does not value or even endorse purity.

UNPACK

- How is sexual impurity pervasive in your world today?
- Why is this so?
- What is so enticing about sexual impurity?

INFORM

- In 1 Corinthians,Paul suggests that sexual sin is one that is committed "against his own body." What do you think he means by this?
- Looking back over the three aspects of The Plan for Purity described above, what does sexual purity for men entail?

LAND

- What issues do you face in the area of personal purity? Why?
- What steps do you need to take to begin to overcome these challenges? How can a mentor or friend help?

DO

- Confess and repent of sexual impurity.
- Develop a plan for purity—identify any additional resources and support needed.

STOP BUILDING A CASE

"A good wife always forgives her husband when she's wrong."
—Milton Berle

"Do not be conformed to this world, but be transformed by the renewal of your mind."
—Romans 12:2

CONSTRUCTING THE CASE

One of the great pivot points in any marriage is that moment when you learn how to stop privately building a case against your wife. Most men will admit that they have a negative sentiment or a privately held cynical belief about their wives. And these don't just pop up overnight but over long periods. What happens is somewhat human, but also dangerous and sinful in a marriage. First, there is some event or a series of events that catalyze into a noticeable negative pattern we don't like. Because of this, we construct a negative opinion of our spouse. Second, to continue building that case, we begin to view them only through this belief and thus interpret unrelated events, comments, or actions as evidence for our positions. We might even think to ourselves when we see supporting evidence, "There it is again." Third—and this is the haymaker—we reinforce these beliefs and pieces of evidence with powerful negative emotions that support the case we've built.

Often these beliefs and portions of evidence arise right in the middle of a heated argument when we feel hurt or disrespected; this is emotional reinforcement for our preconceived notions. And so a negative belief, with supporting evidence and a powerful emotional reinforcement, sears itself deep into our heart, mind, and soul. And this is building a case against our spouse.

Negative Belief + Supporting Evidence + Negative Emotion Event = Case Built Against Our Spouse.

HOW TO DECONSTRUCT THE CASE WE HAVE BUILT
ONE | BECOME AWARE YOU'RE BUILDING THE BIASES

Let's say you hit a point in your marriage where you start to believe that your wife doesn't value your opinion. From then on, anytime she did something without consulting you, you would interpret all those events as evidence for that belief, even if they were innocent and unrelated. Over time, you can imagine how your feelings and attitudes toward her would develop a false construct about her. This is cancerous to a marital relationship. Counselors call this phenomenon confirmation bias.

Many men—and women for that matter—never realize they are constructing these cases. Years into their marriages, they now struggle to deal with issues in their relationship because they've built such a massive case against their spouse. Deconstructing it becomes arduous work because they can only see their spouse through one faulty lens. And many give up because the task of untangling this predicament proves so difficult and is ultimately a fatal blow to the marriage.

To deconstruct the case you've built, you must develop self-awareness. The critical decision is deciding to be aware of what you're constructing. Say to yourself as soon as the negative belief appears, "I'm going to give my spouse the benefit of the doubt." This alone can be ground-breaking self-talk. It will help start the deconstruction process and build momentum in a new direction. It's choosing to interpret events, comments, and actions as having some other reason and purpose besides what you want to believe intuitively. It stops the justification process.

TWO | SIGNALING WITH INFLAMMATORY WORDS OR THOUGHTS

Sometimes when we get baited into building a bias, we use inflammatory language or self-talk like "you always" or "you never." First, "you" is never a great pronoun to use in a heated argument as it's pointed and shaming.

Pronouns like "I" or "me" are much better and focus on your feelings rather than their issues. Second, words like "always" or "never" are almost never accurate. I think it's in our sinful nature to use inflammatory language like this, but it's not helpful. This language is just further proof that you've built a case rather than given your spouse the benefit of the doubt.

And there's your signal. It's the language you think or use that should signal something is off. So when this language arises, use it as a warning signal and begin to pivot your words, thoughts, and actions in a new direction. Romans 12:2 says, "Do not be conformed to this world, but be transformed by the renewal of your mind." I think this applies well to how we think about and worship God, but it has some application in our relationship with our spouses as well. Your inflammatory words and thoughts can be renewed by viewing your wife as she is: the image of God, not your enemy.

THREE | KILL NEGATIVE SOUND BITES AND BUILD POSITIVE ONES

Finally, it might be helpful to write out those negative thoughts and statements you have about your spouse that reinforce the case you've built against her. For example, let's say you're hanging out with your buddies babbling about your respective spouses. Then suddenly the conversation turns negative— what have you instinctively said? "She spends too much." "She's nagging." "She's angry all the time." "She's emotionally needy." These might be indications of what you believe; after all, you wouldn't say it if in some way you didn't believe it. It might be time to write them out, not so you can remember them, but so you can look back objectively on what you think and consider the harm you're inflicting on the person you love.

And as you write it out, list the supporting evidence and kill it. And then renew your mind by considering how God views her. She is "excellent, precious, good, strong, open-handed, loving, caring, blessed, charming, fruitful," and more (Proverbs 31). Begin thinking and speaking of her to your family and others in an honoring way. Even write these words down and repeat them. It's an exercise in gratitude that has the power to help you view her in new ways and build an image and identity of her that might be self-fulfilling. So write down all the things you love about your wife and begin changing and renewing your mind, and maybe hers as well.

REFLECTION & MENTORSHIP

BEGIN

- One of the great pivot points in any marriage is that moment when you learn how to stop privately building a case against your wife.

UNPACK

- What is the greatest challenge you are facing in your marriage today?
- Do you ever talk negatively about this with others? Why?

INFORM

- In Romans, Paul teaches us that renewing the mind is essential. Why?
- What is challenging about the three steps to deconstructing the cases we have built above?

LAND

- What is the case you have built against your spouse?
- How has this impacted your marriage?
- What sound bites do you need to kill?
- What steps do you need to take to view your wife differently?

DO

- Confess the case you have built against your wife and seek forgiveness.
- Pray for your wife each day this week and see her as God sees her.
- Report back how the reconciliation process went.

DIRTY FIGHTING TECHNIQUES

"I am tired of fighting. For once in a while I want to be fought for."

—Unknown.

"A soft answer turns away wrath, but a harsh word stirs up anger."

—Proverbs 15:1

EVENTUALLY, YOU'RE GOING TO FIGHT

In marriage, we are going to encounter conflict, and at some point we're going to fight dirty. And sometimes we will be on the receiving end of these dirty tactics. Perhaps we don't consciously choose to fight in this way. But consciously or unconsciously, we continue to do it because it's worked in the past or because we've seen it modeled. When we fight dirty, we're often looking to gain an advantage through another's weakness. If we're hostile at that moment, we know that we can get a reaction by pushing their buttons in certain areas. We've shifted the goal, now willing to inflict pain to win. And if your goal is to win the argument, there's going to be a loser. Additionally, if you lose a lot, you might even fight dirtier to win occasionally. And thus, the downward cycle that turns ugly. But could there be a better goal than inflicting pain on the other person? Is there a better win?

TWO THINGS TO REMEMBER IN CONFLICT
ONE | THE GOAL OF MARRIAGE

Marriage is not about winning and losing; it's about oneness. When one person in a marriage loses, they both lose, and when one person wins, they both win. Oneness is about a husband and wife becoming so intimately connected that they develop a mental, physical, relational, and spiritual harmony that goes beyond human possibilities. Two become one in the flesh. But occasionally in an effort to find oneness, you and your spouse will have conflict. Conflict is often an attempt to come to mutual understanding. Like two positive poles on a magnet, at times you will repel each other, and when this happens, you will have disagreements, conflicts, arguments, or fights—call them what you want. It's fine to engage in a debate for the purpose of understanding each other and coming to a common understanding. But as these moments happen, you and your spouse can develop some unhealthy patterns. As a result, you might interpret your spouse as an enemy rather than an ally, and therefore go on the attack and fight dirty, losing sight of the goal of understanding.

TWO | STOP DIRTY TACTICS

There are a lot of great dirty fighting techniques out there. Some you know better than others because you use them or have had them used against you. Below is a short list of some common tactics. Consider the ones you use and the one your spouse uses and have a conversation about them. (Please don't have this discussion during a dispute but during a time of peace.) You can even rank them by the ones you feel you each resort to the most.

TWENTY DIRTY TECHNIQUES:

1. **Bad Timing.** Pick the worst time to start an argument.
2. **Escalating.** Move quickly from a single issue to more significant matters you've been waiting to bring up.
3. **Sand Bagging.** Move from the primary issue to all the other problems you have.
4. **Generalizing.** Use inflammatory language like "always" and "never."
5. **Cross-Complaining.** Respond to their complaints with one of your own.

6. **Interrogating.** Imply with a question that they could have easily done something that they didn't do. For example, "Why didn't you..."
7. **Blaming.** Make the issue entirely their fault.
8. **Pulling Rank.** Make the point that you do more than them in every area.
9. **Dominating.** Talk over them regardless of what they say.
10. **Violation Listing.** Recite every injustice you've suffered.
11. **Negative Labeling.** Give the person a negative psychological label like "immature" or "neurotic."
12. **Mind Reading.** Telling the person why they did something even if you don't know.
13. **Predicting.** Predict fatalistic views of the future.
14. **Avoiding Ownership.** Don't take responsibility for anything.
15. **Exiting.** Walk out of the room or leave the house in protest.
16. **Denying Compromise.** Never back down from your position.
17. **Personalizing.** Make it about the person and not the issue.
18. **Victimizing.** Make yourself the eternal martyr.
19. **Grudging.** Hold a grudge forever and bring it up repeatedly.
20. **Shifting.** Be inconsistent in an argument to avert resolution.

REFLECTION & MENTORSHIP
BEGIN

- We all fight dirty at some point, but the point is not to win by fighting dirty—the point is oneness and mutual understanding.

UNPACK

- What dirty fighting did you witness in your home of origin?
- What results did this produce in your family?
- How has your experience impacted your marriage today?

INFORM

- What do you think the word "wrath" means in the Proverb above?
- What dirty techniques do you use?
- What dirty techniques does your spouse use?

LAND

- What issues do you need to address in your fighting techniques?
- What steps do you need to take to find a new way to understand one another?

DO

- Share the list above with your wife and discuss how you each fight dirty in arguments. Be careful not to prescribe her answers.
- Using the steps above, develop a plan together to improve oneness in your marriage.
- If you can, report back with your friend or mentor how this went and what the result was.

SPIRITUAL LEADERSHIP

"There is no such thing as a self-made spiritual leader. A true leader influences others spiritually only because the Spirit works in and through him to a greater degree than in those he leads."

—J. Oswald Sanders

"Likewise, husbands, live with your wives in an understanding way, showing honor to the woman as the weaker vessel, since they are heirs with you of the grace of life, so that your prayers may not be hindered."

—1 Peter 3:7

THE CHALLENGE OF LEADING AT HOME

Spiritual leadership in the home is one of our primary environments of leadership and by far the most challenging. It's often a hard topic for men to even talk about because they don't know what to do or how to do it, have failed in attempts, or just lacked a healthy model in their home of origin. Combine this with the shame some men perceive from their spouse, children, and pastors, compounded with feelings of underperformance, and many give up. But giving up is not the right response; therefore, we must find good ways to grab hold of the baton we have so willingly dropped. We are called to lead in our homes but having the right spirit and doing it in the right way is very important.

PRINCIPLES ON LEADING AT HOME
ONE | CORRECTLY UNDERSTAND STRONG LEADERSHIP

To become the man God wants you to be, you need to be a strong leader in your home. And "strong leader" does not entail a domineering, demanding, dictatorial, presence. A strong leader is humble both in spirit and in God-centered, confident will. He is a man who finds ways to influence his family by being a servant, not a dictator. Like Jesus, he will find ways to be strong when required and soft when needed. With each person in his home, he must find a voice that will influence and persuade, winning them over to God's will, not his own. As men, we are called to lead, but we should assert strength without breaking the spirits of those under our leadership. Sometimes strength demands a soft tone, subtle persuasion, and cunning wisdom that will entice a person toward God's will. Either way, this requires deep strength and personal confidence.

TWO | YOU'RE NOT SPIRITUALLY RESPONSIBLE, BUT YOU ARE SPIRITUALLY OBLIGATED

We should always feel a great responsibility for the spiritual leadership of our home. As men, we feel an almost natural impulse to provide, and provision for our family is essential. God wants us to work to produce food, shelter, clothing, and basic needs. He has modeled this for us as the first provider. But we cannot limit this to natural provision. To provide for only a family's physical needs is to miss the greatest need: spiritual provision. And as our heavenly Father provided spiritually for us, we are called to provide spiritually for our family. But we must be careful because while we are responsible **to** our family spiritually, we are not responsible **for** our family spiritually. We are called to train and teach, but we cannot force anyone to believe in God. And this creates an unusual tension in spiritual leadership. We can pray and prepare, but we cannot push anyone to grow or believe in Jesus Christ. And it is often for this reason that many feel like a failure. But we should never misinterpret our roles when it comes to our spiritual responsibility. We are entirely responsible for our own choices, and we are also fully accountable for teaching and training, but we are not responsible for the independent decisions the people in our household make—even when we feel otherwise.

THREE | SANCTIFY YOUR WIFE

One of the great calls in spiritual leadership for the husband is to love his wife as Christ loved the church. And the way He did it was sacrificially, sanctifying her "by the washing of water with the word" (Eph. 5:25). Too many times we see ourselves in competition with our wives' leadership, or we are combative with her. But this is not the work of a husband. We are commanded to wash our wives in truth from God's Word, not beat them into submission. This requires a humility that recognizes you are not the truth— God is. Thus, you need to drive her to His truth, not yours.

FOUR | EMBRACE TEACHABLE MOMENTS BUT DON'T PREACH

Most men fail miserably at the first attempt of spiritual leadership. Maybe we think we should present a regular sermon to our family like those we receive at church. This is a commonly held misconception that you may be embarrassed to admit. While I know a few families that hold intermittent worship and devotional times with their families, many men feel ill-equipped to lead these. And to be honest, most family members would rather not endure them. So instead, why not turn available moments into teachable moments. Take every moment you do have to share praise, take the opportunity to teach, share a moment from your past, or process something you are reading in God's Word. This does require active spiritual engagement and discipline, but that's good for you too.

FIVE | IT'S ONE MOMENT AT A TIME

Think of leadership one moment at a time. Consider each day how you can spur your family on toward love and good deeds. Refuse to see it as one moment and embrace it as a lifestyle of many moments. Your family will remember the insignificant things you do far more than those planned moments. Like the prayer in the car. The hug in the doorway. The prayer you prayed with them by phone. A listening ear. A thoughtful email. Help with homework. Each of these moments has the divine opportunity just teed up for us by God. Do one thing to lead your family spiritually.

REFLECTION & MENTORSHIP
BEGIN

- Spiritual leadership in the home is one of our primary environments of leadership and by far the most challenging.

UNPACK

- Describe spiritual leadership in your home as a child.
- How have your past experiences with spiritual leadership impacted you today?

INFORM

- Peter teaches us many lessons about the spiritual leadership of our wives; what are the lessons?
- What life-giving lessons can you take away from the five points above?

LAND

- How would you rate your current spiritual leadership skills? Why?
- What issues do you face as you engage in spiritual leadership?
- What steps do you need to take to overcome these issues?

DO

- Identify your personal goals and desires for spiritual leadership and share them with a friend or mentor.
- Take a step toward your spiritual leadership goals in small ways each day this week.

INFLUENTIAL FATHERS

"It is easier to build strong children than to repair broken men."
—Frederick Douglass

"This is my beloved Son, with whom I am well pleased."
—Matthew 3:17

CHILDREN NEED FATHERS

Children need a male influence in the home. And by influence, we do not mean just an occasional appearance or a buddy dad, but a deliberate father. While presence is a part of fathering, and sometimes children need a friend who will listen, fathering is intentional and requires a lifetime of commitment. It doesn't happen by accident even though we may have felt accidentally thrust into it. And so fathering requires some strategy. It's a decision and commitment.

THREE FATHERING APPROACHES
ONE | THE PRODUCER DAD

This is the father who is always doing something at work or home because he values provision and is very committed to it. Provision for his family is his principal purpose but sometimes to the exclusion of providing the one thing his family needs most: relationship. Unfortunately, he can work himself to death to provide food, finance, and fun for his family. Sometimes he's so consumed with producing he appears distant and preoccupied, but in his mind, it's for a good reason. Driven by a deep desire to succeed, this father has an approach his children perceive as "present but absent." His spouse and children know he cares but in a way that lacks a necessary component. This can leave the family emotionally disconnected from their husband and father despite his drive.

TWO | THE BUDDY DAD

The second type of father is the buddy dad. He is perpetually present at dance recitals and football games and appears to live vicariously through the life and accomplishments of his children. He wants to "be a bud" to the exclusion of parenting his children. He may feel that the best way to relate to his children is to support them by being like them. So when his kids' friends are over, he acts like them, plays like them, and jokes like them. And while there's nothing wrong with being jovial, acting like a juvenile to connect is not good fatherly behavior. Many fathers who exclusively resort to this technique do so because they lack the understanding of how to lead as a father. In the end, this leaves the spouse and children wanting for more. He may be popular for the moment, but his actions fail to produce dividends as his children have children of their own. And the cycle of buddying up to his children is repeated by the next generation. Remember, what you win your children with is what you win them to.

THREE | THE DELIBERATE DAD

And then finally, there is the best model. It's the father that is a producer (within limits) and a bud (also within limits), but also deliberate. He's observant and aware of what's going on in his children's lives. He may seem a little invasive at times, but it's not just to find out what they are doing wrong—he also wants to see what they are doing right. Deliberate dads want to know how their children are handling challenges, selecting friends, building relationships, setting goals, and traversing spiritual difficulties. You need to know all of these things in order to be able to coach your children effectively.

You need to find ways to be deliberate, and not deliberately annoying, but consciously connected and deliberately directive. This is the intentional father. He's not just reactive in traumatic events that become teachable moments, but he seeks proactive opportunities to lead and direct. And this requires engagement, forethought, and planning, which is work—some of the most important work you will do for about twenty critical years. And from child to child, this requires a situational engagement that is specific to each that will woo them into successful independence and adulthood.

REFLECTION & MENTORSHIP

BEGIN

- A father that influences is one that values producing, cultivates friendship, and deliberately helps his children to navigate toward adulthood.

UNPACK

- Using the three descriptions above, what, if any, describe your experience in your home of origin?
- How would you describe the type of dad you would like to be?

INFORM

- Every son wants to hear the words that God offered His Son, "This is my beloved Son, with whom I am well pleased." Have you heard these words from your father?
- How would you like to be more deliberate as a dad?

LAND

- What issues are preventing you from becoming more deliberate?
- What steps do you need to take to become more deliberate?

DO

- Identify one deliberate action you can take with each of your children this week.
- Report back to your mentor or discussion partner the impact these actions had on your children and on you.

SITUATIONAL ENGAGEMENT AS A FATHER

"Anyone can be a father, but it takes someone special to be a dad, and that's why I call you Dad because you are so special to me. You taught me the game and you taught me how to play it right."

—Wade Boggs

"Fathers, do not provoke your children to anger, but bring them up in the discipline and instruction of the Lord."

—Ephesians 6:4

FATHERING, THE GREAT ADVENTURE

Becoming a father is one of the greatest adventures. In this moment, our identity and title forever change. Some of us are thrust into it, and others of us planned it; either way, it's an adventure. Throughout Scripture, we see many different types of fathers and the positive or negative wake their legacy left behind. Take for example King Saul, in whom we see the Abusive Father; he had moments of embittered anger toward his son Jonathan (1 Samuel 20:30). In King David, we see the Absent Father who was absorbed in his ventures and therefore missed opportunities with his children (2 Sam 13:21). In High Priest Eli, we note the Abandoned Father who abdicated his leadership and failed to address his sons' need for correction and direction (1 Samuel 2:22).

In Abraham, we see the image of the Appointed Father; through his incredible faith, he became the model man, leader, and husband (Genesis 18:19). In Noah, we see the Adventurous Father who despite challenges and obstacles plowed through hardship and led his family to safety and victory (Genesis 7:13–14). And we even have the Audacious Stepfather in Joseph who in a vision discovered his calling and became the human caretaker for the God of the Universe, Jesus Christ (Matthew 1:20). Regardless of the type of earthly father we have, we feel his wake, and our children will experience ours. The question remains, how can we be the best father to the children God has given us?

If you take the time as a father to observe your children, you will discover that they are each unique and respond to life in unique ways. You will notice how they respond to crises, how they make decisions, what entertains them, and what kinds of friendships they build. At each stage of development through infancy, childhood, adolescence, and the young adult years, you are going to witness varying levels of competence and confidence that require you to parent in different ways. The key is understanding how to engage your children individually, situationally, and strategically so that you can give them great advice and be the best dad possible. Here are a few things to keep in mind.

THREE KEYS TO BEING A STRATEGIC FATHER
ONE | EACH CHILD IS INDIVIDUALLY DIFFERENT

Every child in your home is going to be different and needs a different kind of love, coaching, directing, and challenging. Some kids need to be pushed. Some need to be loved. Some need to be disciplined—yes, my wife and I had one we disciplined more than others. Maybe you were that son. Regardless, God creates each one different and yet still in His image. These young image-bearers, therefore, are going to have different personalities, gifts, talents, temperaments, styles, and relationships through life.

Because they will go through rapid change through their youth, they will also experience certain stimuli, pressures, and physical changes that will be overwhelming for them—and for you too. While you are going to want each of your children to act the same, grow the same, mature the same, and believe the same, they won't. Often, we fail to remember this, and thus our expectations of them are unrealistic, which adds undue pressure for them and for you. The hope you should have is one for change. For as soon as you get familiar with one challenge in a child's life, be prepared for the change that might individually unravel you.

TWO | EACH CHILD IS SITUATIONALLY DIFFERENT

From one child to the next, children are going to be situationally a little different. Some of your children will learn faster, and others slower. Some will be ultra-responsible, and others won't. Some will be orderly, and others a little messy. Some will be smarter, and others not so much. Some will have a physical ability, and others will be a little bit klutzy. We must also prepare for this. It can be a bit irritating when you realize you must expand your parenting methods, but again, this is God's design. This leads to the third and critical point.

THREE | EACH CHILD NEEDS A STRATEGIC FATHERING APPROACH

As fathers, our end goal is to move our children from dependence to independence. Or maybe it's better said that we want them to move from dependence on their earthly father to interdependence on their heavenly Father. Keeping this in mind, we need to embrace a strategy that supports this process. But we also need one that incorporates individual and situational differences. And here's a strategy that can help. Consider your role and engagement with each child and situation through the lens of one of four roles: director, coach, supporter, and observer.

Every situation and child will at some point need one of these four fathering approaches. These correspond to different involvement levels moving from very involved to less involved. First, a father who is a director is one who tells it like it is. He commands, directs, and determines the direction. There are times we are called to direct as men, leaders, husbands, and fathers. We should not be directing all the time, but certain times demand this level of involvement. Out of concern for injury, at the emergence of spiritual issues, or at the threat of future danger, we may need to direct.

Second, sometimes as a father we need to coach. A coach teaches, observes, and redirects. You set a game plan, train to that plan, watch it unfold, and redirect as needed to help your children gain a win for the team. You need to demonstrate how the parts connect to the whole at each step so they can obtain a complete understanding of what success entails and what their role in the process is.

Third is the father who is a supporter. Strategically, this father is progressively less involved. He may offer verbal, emotional, intellectual, and spiritual support but is circumstantially unengaged. And fourth is the observer. This father is more like a cheerleader in the stands and is mostly unengaged, viewing his child from afar. Each of these strategies must be deployed at a different time, in different situations, with individual children. And this is what makes being a father hard; it requires us to be on our best game at home, being the kind of father that our children need at that precise moment—with the goal of moving them from dependence to independence to interdependence on God.

Frankly, each of us will find that one or another of these styles is our own default. For example, some of us are directors all the time. But this is never good for winning our children over. The worst thing you can do to a child is come on full force in the style of a director when they need a coach or maybe just some fatherly support. I guess you could phrase it "situational engagement" because sometimes we're called to use different fatherly approaches strategically depending on the circumstances. So you can be a director one day, but you can also be a coach the next. Or you can be an observer or a supporter, depending on the readiness of your children and their competence and confidence in the tasks and issues before them.

You may start out as a director, hoping to shift into becoming a supporter one small step at a time. Sometimes you will need to increase your engagement, and other times you will need to decrease it. Either way, using these approaches for strategic engagement and knowing how to use them over time will help you to be the father your children need at the time, thereby building up their competence and confidence. Remember, being strategic means being open to a change and moving dynamically. It's not as complicated as it may initially sound; once you start practicing this strategic approach, it will become second nature to you.

# REFLECTION & MENTORSHIP
BEGIN

- The key to fathering is understanding how to engage children individually, situationally, and strategically so that you can give them great advice and be the best dad for them at that given moment.

UNPACK

- What is easy for you about fathering?
- What is challenging for you as a father?
- How would you describe your own father?

INFORM

- In Ephesians 6:4, we are given limits as a father. What is the limit? Why are we given it?
- What is challenging about being a strategic father?

LAND

- How can you be more strategic?
- What steps do you need to take with your children at this time, and how does this differ child by child?

DO

- Take a strategic approach with each of your children this week.
- Report back to your mentor or discussion partner on how this impacted your children and your leadership.

GUIDING THE PRODIGAL CHILD

"Children begin by loving their parents; as they grow older they judge them; sometimes they forgive them."

—Oscar Wilde

"And he arose and came to his father. But while he was still a long way off, his father saw him and felt compassion, and ran and embraced him and kissed him."

—Luke 15:20

THE CHALLENGE OF PRODIGAL CHILDREN

There are few challenges more difficult or more common than dealing with a wayward child. It's frustrating, tests our limits emotionally, drives us to prayer, and can even leave us feeling like a failure. Many parents experience feelings of shame and regret when they compare themselves and their children to others. These are hard seasons of life, but they can be weathered. Here are some markers for you to remember if or when that season comes.

FOUR THINGS TO REMEMBER FOR THE PARENT OF A PRODIGAL

ONE | REMEMBER THEIR FAILURE IS NOT YOUR FAILURE

When your children reach the age where they begin to make their own decisions, this should remind you that they are an independent creation of God. Each child is unique, with distinct wiring, challenges, and encounters that will shape his or her life. Often in error, you will want to compare your experiences as a youth to your child's, but each of our experiences is unique. As you did, your kids will make their own decisions, and in the transition from childhood to adulthood, they will start making independent choices that will result in great pain for them and you. While you will foresee the consequences of these decisions and issue a warning, your children will insist, ignore, and incite choices that will not match up with values you embrace. This is sometimes devastating.

During this time, you should be careful about comparing your child to other kids who appear to have their lives together. In reality, these other kids probably have their own struggles and problems. Know that God has a plan for your child. He knew that they would choose the direction they have chosen and still loves them deeply. This season is going to be tempting for you as well. You might experience this sinking feeling of losing ground and influence over your child. While at some point they will move from dependence to independence, the way we imagine it is not always the way it happens.

Also, it is going to be tempting to live in shame as other parents might appear to be critical or judgmental. Treat their comments or criticisms as mere misunderstandings. They have not walked in your shoes. Surround yourself with parents and friends who will encourage, support, and love you—people who want to treat your child with respect and love based on the truth of God's Word. Remember, there are no perfect families, kids, or parents.

TWO | REMEMBER TOUGH LOVE

Sometimes it's necessary to take tough but critical action with a prodigal child, such as when a behavior threatens others or himself. This is especially true when the child is living under your rule, roof, and resources. Tough love is a parenting decision that promotes God-honoring choices, choices that enforce certain constraints that cause a child to take responsibility for his actions; tough love is not a tactic for getting your way or exerting command. God never wants us to provoke our children but rather to guide, persuade, and direct them.

Choose your battles wisely, as not everything demands tough love. Weigh the issues carefully and decide what sort of response is appropriate. If your child is struggling with dishonesty, drugs, or persistent disobedience, he may be in need of tougher love at this moment. Be thoughtful, calm, and less reactive. Sometimes children make choices to elicit a reactive response from parents, hoping to expose your reasoning and emotion.

The most powerful tool that you have as a parent is love—unconditional and tough. No child will ignore your love, even though at the moment it may feel like she is doing just that. As you find all kinds of ways to love your child through her rebellion, it will not be forgotten or go unnoticed.

THREE | REMEMBER TO REMAIN IN A RELATIONSHIP

Perhaps the biggest mistake parents make in parenting a prodigal is forfeiting the relationship. Remember that God never does this. He is patient, loving, merciful, and graceful to a fault. To the extent that you can, always stay in a relationship regardless of your child's choices. While God hates sin, He loves sinners, and you are one too. Somehow, He was patient with you. And you need to embrace this same patience with your children. By retaining relational capital, you leave the door open for future grace.

FOUR | REMEMBER THE PARENT AND PRODIGAL WILL BOTH BE TRANSFORMED

Consider this: Franklin Graham, the son of Billy Graham, fits the description of a prodigal. Read his story sometime; it's the story of the Prodigal Son. God used his prodigal experiences to make Franklin and Billy into better men. God uses the circumstances of our lives to mold and shape us in different ways. Some will take the path of Billy Graham and some the path of Franklin Graham. But as parents, we too are transformed. We need to continue to believe, trust, and have faith that God can redeem anything, including us, through these experiences. We learn what it is to love when it's hard, to dispense grace when we want to deliver judgment, and to wait in a relationship when we desire to cast it off. Prodigal children often transform us through a process of personal trial. In this, we become more like Christ.

Henri J. Nouwen wrote an insightful book on this subject called *The Return of the Prodigal Son*. If you are in this situation, get a copy and breathe deep into God's grace. Build a prayer team around you that will pray for you and your prodigal. Often God has two plans in these situations—one for you and one for your child.

REFLECTION & MENTORSHIP

BEGIN

- We have all been prodigals, but parenting one is a challenge like no other. Yet how you respond has the power to reshape you and your child.

UNPACK

- When you were a child, how did you specifically test your parents?
- Why do children test their parents? Knowing this, how should a parent appropriately respond?

INFORM

- Luke 15:20 marks a very emotional moment in the story of the Prodigal Son. What is powerful or unusual about this moment?
- If you have a prodigal child, what stirs you about the four points above?
- If you do not have a prodigal child, what concerns you about the four points above?

LAND

- What issues do you need to address as a father?
- What steps do you need to take to show love to your prodigal child?

DO

- After identifying your issues and steps above, execute your plan.

STEPFAMILY FUNDAMENTALS

"The first step to a healthy remarriage is you. Is this a surprise? Life wounds all of us. The losses, disappointments, and hurts of life will not heal themselves—you must choose to heal."

—Jeff and Judi Parziale

"Is not this the carpenter, the son of Mary and brother of James and Joses and Judas and Simon? And are not his sisters here with us?"

—Mark 6:3

IT'S A FAMILY IN A BLENDER

There is no better word to describe the blended family than "blended." When we consider the challenges of this new family unit, it can often feel like you've been thrown in a blender—stirred, chopped, sliced, and beaten to a pulp. The variety of different opinions, philosophies, and approaches coming together at one time frequently contributes to the confusion and chaos. Some days you will barely be able to hold it together. After all, you and your spouse were brought together by love, but only after navigating the trauma of a divorce or death—and perhaps some healing is yet to come for you or other members of your family.

Meanwhile, a new household needs to be established, and your parents, children, and even extended families may have all kinds of opinions on the relationships involved and how they should work. Old patterns, to some extent, will need to be unlearned, and some new models will be invented. This can be especially complicated for children. Familiar with one parenting style, they now have to learn another; the learning curve is only steepened if both biological parents remarry. And thus, this change is challenging for all involved. Both parents and children are likely to experience confusion and frustration at times.

FOUR PRINCIPLES TO KEEP IN MIND
ONE | IT'S GOING TO TAKE TIME

Husbands and wives are required to make each other a priority; this is hard in a newly blended family. It may take extra effort to work through differences, so don't just storm out of the room physically or emotionally—lean into the conflict. Different parenting styles are going to clash, and former patterns that worked might end up changing into something new and different. These changes are uncomfortable for everyone. It's going to take time to recognize, agree on, and build this new family system. In the meantime, show respect and kindness. Learn from your partner and listen to her. Create opportunities to brainstorm ideas on making your marriage and family function better. It takes time, but the wait is so worth it.

TWO | WITH CHILDREN, LET THE BIOLOGICAL PARENT LEAD FOR A SEASON

Upon a divorce or the death of a parent, a child's world turns upside down. If you think about it, they are along for a ride that they did not ask to be taken on. This amount of change is unsettling for them emotionally, intellectually, and spiritually. They need some things to remain unchanged, and one that can be constant is the voice of their biological parent in moments of stress, teaching, redirection, or discipline. So let your wife take the lead in parenting her biological children. You may not always agree with her method of discipline or how she delivers it, but you can respect the choices of your spouse. Over time, the hope is that all your children will learn to respect and love the joint discipline of both parents, biological or not.

THREE | CREATE NEW METHODS AND MEMORIES

There are so many great methods and memories you will struggle to import. This always surprises couples in the new blended family. We assume that everyone will love our old traditions because we thought they were so wonderful and had so many wonderful memories attached to them. And of course, we are shocked when the new family system abhors them. You will have to craft new traditions, and it is going to take time for these ideas to catch on as your new family members accept them as their own. But be patient and hang in there. You are starting over, and with this restart is the opportunity to forge new patterns, new memories, and new methods of life together within this new family that God has assembled. So get creative and start building.

FOUR | GOD CAN DO EXTRAORDINARY WORK IN A BLENDED FAMILY

Consider the case of Moses, son of Jochebed, who was born into an Israelite family in Egyptian slavery. Yet for his safety, he was sent down the Nile River in a basket when the Pharaoh of Egypt called for the mass genocide of all the Israelite boys. His parents, who trusted God, discovered that Moses made his way into the hands of Queen Bithia, Pharaoh's daughter, and was raised in this royal home.

For the first 40 years of his life, Moses grew up in extreme wealth and luxury as a stepchild to the Pharaoh. This was Moses' stepfamily. Then Moses discovered his Israelite heritage and fled the comfort of this palatial home to discover another home. Later, he headed to Midian, where he established an intimate relationship with God and married Zipporah, the daughter of Jethro.

After another 40 years, Moses left the desert and returned to Egypt as a prophet and leader to free the Israelite nation from captivity, leading them to 40 years of wandering in the desert. There he shepherded a nation of people in hopes of leading them into the land of promise. So think about that for a minute. Moses was a kid who grew up in a stepfamily yet became a father and the leader of God's people—the man whom God used to lead His people from slavery and through whom God delivered the Law on Mount Sinai. I would say that is a pretty spectacular story of redemption and hope for all stepfamilies.

So keep in mind that while the process may be difficult for a while, God has something special for a blended family. And if you have one, you might be raising a future leader of God's people right now.

REFLECTION & MENTORSHIP

BEGIN

- When two adults are brought together by love following either a divorce or death, the challenges are numerous—but not without hope for a better future.

UNPACK

- Was your family of origin marked by divorce, death, or remarriage? If so, what was challenging about this for you? What lessons did you learn through this experience?
- If your family of origin was not marked by divorce, death, or remarriage, what made your parents' marriage work?
- Do you have any lingering concerns or insecurities related to your previous marriage? Did you have any anxiety about remarrying? How so?

INFORM

- Jesus grew up in a stepfamily; what's interesting about this theologically and practically?
- Clearly, the crowds found the nature of Jesus' family interesting. Why?
- Of the four principles above, which one stands out to you?

LAND

- What challenges do you face in your current marriage that you need to address?
- What do you need to remember and what steps do you need to take to be a husband, father, and leader in your home?

DO

- Pray for your family each day this week.
- Through discussion and prayer,identify one new tradition you will build with your spouse.
- Talk about it with your blended family.
- Execute the plan and report back to a friend or mentor how this exercise impacted you.

THE ULTIMATE LEADERSHIP CHALLENGE

"A man should never neglect his family for business."

—*Walt Disney*

"You shall teach them diligently to your children, and shall talk of them when you sit in your house, and when you walk by the way, and when you lie down, and when you rise."

—*Deuteronomy 6:7*

THE GREAT LEADERSHIP OPPORTUNITY

One of the greatest privileges of being a father and husband is the opportunity you'll have in leading your family. At the same time, it's one of those responsibilities that leaves men feeling inadequate. Many of you feel this way because you lacked a model of leadership in your home of origin, or perhaps the challenges are just more complex than you anticipated. Despite this, there are few things more important than leading your family well. All husbands and fathers are called to lead in both their marriages and family. But what does this mean? And how are you to do it?

The truth is that good leadership doesn't happen by accident. It requires a deliberate investment of yourself into the people in your home.

THREE CRITICAL INVESTMENTS OF FAMILY LEADERSHIP
ONE | LEADING YOURSELF IS LEADING YOUR FAMILY

Husbands and fathers only lead well when they have paid careful attention to their character. We're always leading from both our wounds and our wins. Therefore, you cannot lead well when you have not addressed both. Your wounds are especially important because they shape who you are and thus impact others in powerful ways. The goal is to address wounds to become a man of virtue and character grounded in and shaped by Christ.

Your emotional, spiritual, relational, and physical well-being determines the force and impact of your leadership. You must learn to lead yourself before you can influence others, especially your family. After all, they know you better than any other person, so you won't be able to hide even small character flaws from them. Your life is their model, and they will be following your lead. To lead your family intentionally, you need to have a plan for yourself. Ask yourself the question: "Do I have a plan for my development and growth as a man, husband, and father?" If not, you better get one, because your leadership is only as good as your plan—and subsequently how you work that plan.

TWO | A NURTURING MARRIAGE IS LEADERSHIP

Families are built around relationships, and the relationship most visible to children is the one between their parents. Children pay a great deal of attention to the interactions, emotional connection, and closeness of their mother and father. If you stop to reflect, you know exactly how healthy your parents' relationship is and how that health, or lack of it, impacted you. Everything you do to nurture your marriage relationship will have an impact on the health of your family as a whole, including how you love, honor, respect, listen to, and forgive your spouse. So nurture her more than even your children—she is, after all, your second-most-important relationship behind only God—and then watch how this slowly impacts the force of your leadership over time.

THREE | INVESTING IN YOUR CHILDREN
BUILDS LEADERSHIP INFLUENCE

Winston Churchill, the great British leader, had a father who was disconnected from him. In fact, his father's dairy had a notation to this effect: "Spent the day fishing with Winston. A day wasted." I suspect that Winston Churchill spent his life trying to prove his worth to his father.

Never underestimate the power of even simple investments in the life of your kids. While we don't want to worship our children, we do need to invest in them. Your kids want to know that you love them, and investing time in them demonstrates this. You can only lead those with whom you have a relationship, so as an invested father, you are investing in leadership. And over time, the influence of your leadership will grow. This is why Jesus spent so much time with His disciples.

Your impact on your children's current and future life will be directly impacted by your investment of time, especially when they are between the ages of 4–16. This short window of time in your life is not something you will ever get back, once the time is spent. Therefore, invest it by attending their games, concerts, and events. Be present with them in pursuits that matter to them. Engage casually with them, take them for one-on-one dinners, ask them for prayer requests and pray for them, extend grace to them when needed, show them how to do something new, build something, work on a car with them, or have a significant talk with them on a controversial topic. From time to time, ask them their "high and low of the day" and discover their challenges and disappointments. And then, finally, share your experiences with them, especially your failures. As you do, they will catch your values, beliefs, and faith. It may not manifest instantly, but its impact will be felt in the future. All of this translates into leadership in your home.

REFLECTION & MENTORSHIP
BEGIN
- One of the greatest privileges of a father and husband is the opportunity you'll have in leading your family.

UNPACK
- Describe your father's leadership. How did this positively and negatively impact you?
- Describe your parents' relationship. How did this positively and negatively impact you?

INFORM

- Deuteronomy 6:7 is a command for fathers. What is the mandate?
- How would you evaluate your leadership in the three areas above?

LAND

- What issues need to be addressed in your family leadership?
- What steps do you need to take to address these issues?

DO

- Using the answers from the "Land" section, create a plan of action to lead better as a husband and father.
- Give a friend or mentor permission to keep you accountable to the plan.

FAILING AS A FATHER

"When I was a boy of 14, my father was so ignorant I could hardly stand to have the old man around. But when I got to be 21, I was astonished at how much the old man had learned in seven years."

—Mark Twain

"Fathers, do not provoke your children, lest they become discouraged."

—Colossians 3:21

WE'VE ALL FAILED

I don't know any father or husband who doesn't feel like he has failed on numerous occasions. This feeling of failure can cascade out of control and further prevent you from being the leader God wants you to be in the home. When we experience feelings of inadequacy, we sometimes engage in self-shame to reinforce our initial failure. While this shaming cycle may appear to help, it's only another manifestation of indirect pride that says, "I'm no good and a complete failure" rather than "I'm a redeemed man, husband, and father who has simply made another mistake."

While the voice of shame wants men, husbands, and fathers to ruminate perpetually in their failures, a man of God refuses to live in this state. By the power of the Spirit of God, he will instead get up and give it another go, attempting daily to live out his new and present identity in Christ—rejecting his former way of life one failure at a time. Sometimes it helps to have a strategy for those times we blow it.

FIVE THINGS TO KEEP IN MIND WHEN YOU FAIL AS A FATHER
ONE | EVERY FATHER FAILS

While men tend not to talk about their failures much, especially regarding their children, we do fail—and sometimes frequently. This is because the call of being of a father is not one many men were prepared for. Most learn to be a better father through their failure. Here's what this might look like:

- Anger that was deliberately hurtful
- Sharp or inflammatory statements that inflict pain
- Self-absorption that left a child needing relationship
- Insensitivity to a child's present issues
- Under-involvement due to obsessive overworking
- Emotional or physical absence that alienates

Over the last few days, you were probably implicit in one of these actions. That's because they are common failures. And when done perpetually, they have a damaging and sometimes long-lasting impact on children. But how can we overcome the failure and the effect of the failure?

TWO | BE MORE AWARE OF YOUR AREAS OF WEAKNESS

Every man has areas of vulnerability based on his unique wiring. Some struggle with impatience and anger. Others struggle to guard their attitudes and words, or to be present in the moment. And still others consistently put work ahead of family and marriage. A way to become more aware of those vulnerabilities is to reflect on them by journaling. Writing your thoughts down has a way of imprinting the problem and potential solutions to memory. Mapping out more positive outcomes might be more helpful than wallowing in regret, shame, and self-defeat. In essence, what you're doing is making a plan for the next time you are faced with a similar situation. The more aware you are of your proclivities, the less likely you are to repeat the bad behaviors that are linked to them.

THREE | INVITE THE SPIRIT'S WORK

Ask the Holy Spirit to remind you when you are tempted to go off the rails. The Apostle Paul tells us in Romans 8:26–27, "Likewise the Spirit helps us in our weakness. For we do not know what to pray for as we ought, but the

Spirit himself intercedes for us with groanings too deep for words. And he who searches hearts knows what is the mind of the Spirit, because the Spirit intercedes for the saints according to the will of God."

There are two things you need to know about the Spirit of God who lives within you. First, the Spirit supports you in your weaknesses. And second, He mediates with the Father on your behalf. Because the Spirit's ministry is to help us become more like Christ, He will remind us if we ask Him to help us in our areas of weakness. Ask Him each day to help you be aware of those situations where you can quickly go off the rails as a father; this will make a huge difference. And you will notice He will help as requested.

FOUR | SEEK AND MODEL FORGIVENESS

Your ego is your enemy. Asking forgiveness means that you have to admit to the one you wronged that you failed. Arrogance keeps us from admitting failure and makes us overly concerned about contrition being interpreted as weakness. Ironically, that's not how others perceive us when we ask for forgiveness. They see the courage to ask forgiveness as an act of strength and humility—an action of a father who wants to change and grow.

In the egoless transaction of asking for and receiving forgiveness, relationships are healed, understanding increases, and the Spirit is overjoyed. Never underestimate the power of confession and forgiveness. Some of the great moments of fatherhood are found in the moments we seek our children's forgiveness. While this is hard, there are few actions more healing than admitting our failure to them and seeking forgiveness from God with them.

FIVE | PLAN TO BE A BETTER FATHER

Healthy relationships, marriages, and families don't happen by accident. They happen because you're intentional. Here are the essential questions: What is your plan as a father to grow your family this year? Just as important, what is your plan to improve yourself as a father? What goals have you set for your family? How will you help them as a father? How will you remind yourself of those goals so that they don't get lost in the busyness of life? What other men have you shared your plan with who can encourage you and pray for you? These are essential questions, and most fathers never consider them. Remember, you can either live intentionally or accidentally. Don't settle for the odds of an accidental life but pursue the success of an intentional life—and so determine a plan.

And if you have failed, remember these words of Theodore Roosevelt:

"It is not the critic who counts; not the man who points out how the strong man stumbles, or where the doer of deeds could have done them better. The credit belongs to the man who is actually in the arena, whose face is marred by dust and sweat and blood; who strives valiantly; who errs, who comes short again and again, because there is no effort without error and shortcoming; but who does actually strive to do the deeds; who knows great enthusiasms, the great devotions; who spends himself in a worthy cause; who at the best knows in the end the triumph of high achievement, and who at the worst, if he fails, at least fails while daring greatly, so that his place shall never be with those cold and timid souls who neither know victory nor defeat."

Get up, dust off, and get back into the fight.

REFLECTION & MENTORSHIP
BEGIN
- Every father fails; the key is to get back up and give it another go in your identity in Christ.

UNPACK
- When your father failed, did his admit his failure to you? What is your best guess as to why he did or didn't?
- How do you currently respond to failure with your children?

INFORM
- What does it mean to "not provoke" in Colossians 3:21?
- How does "provoking" lead to discouragement?
- What does discouragement look like in your children?
- Of the five points above, which challenges you today?

LAND

- What issue do you need to address with your children today?
- What steps do you need to take to address this issue?

DO

- Talk to your children about one thing you would like to do differently with them.
- Report back to your mentor or discussion partner on how this went.

DISCIPLINING WITH WISDOM

"As wonderful as they were, my parents didn't teach me anything about self-discipline, concentration, patience, or focus. If I hadn't had a family myself, I probably never would've done anything. Marriage taught me responsibility."

—Dick Van Dyke

"Children, obey your parents in the Lord, for this is right. Honor your father and mother (this is the first commandment with a promise), that it may go well with you and that you may live long in the land. Fathers, do not provoke your children to anger, but bring them up in the discipline and instruction of the Lord."

—Ephesians 6:1–4

DISCIPLINE IS CHALLENGING TO NAVIGATE

Understanding how to discipline a child requires a lot of wisdom, sometimes more than you feel like you possess. If you are too harsh, you could end up intimidating your children emotionally and thus hijacking their ability to learn through the discipline. But on the other hand, if you are too lenient, you may risk removing the guardrails that provide boundaries and protection for your children in the present and down the road.

You may also be intimidated by the idea that your children's view of their heavenly Father is directly influenced by their biological father; how you discipline them has the power to either drive them away from or closer to God. A harsh biological father can generate imagery of a harsh heavenly Father—even though this is uncharacteristic of God. On the other hand, a compassionate biological father can draw attention to the compassion and love of the heavenly Father. Regardless, you steward something so special when you are given children, and stewardship requires the use of discipline. And your interactions with your children in the heat of this discipline need to reflect the character and person of Christ.

As the apostle Paul reminds families in the Ephesian church, there is a promise attached to obeying and honoring your father and mother: "that it may go well with you and that you may live long in the land." As Paul invites attention to the Law given on Mt. Sinai, he is reminding us of God's intended promises for children who learn how to honor and obey their parents in the Lord. This is important not only for children to remember but for parents to understand. Children must "learn" (the operative word) to honor and obey God, and it is not a natural instinct.

Disobedience and dishonor come naturally; therefore, we must learn to honor and obey all authority in life (work and government included). And we learn to do this first in our home. In fact, how we honor and obey our parents will be reflected in how we honor and obey others in life. Generally, those who have not learned to do so at home may be challenged throughout their lives when faced with boundaries in other areas. Learned discipline as a child leads to better self-discipline in the future. And it all begins at home, with you as the father. It all starts with parents who wisely and lovingly establish boundaries with their children and, when necessary, help them stay within those boundaries through discipline. Teach your children to honor and obey within limits set by you at different stages of their lives; this has a lifelong impact.

The need for discipline that teaches honor and obedience is balanced by Paul's admonition to fathers, "Do not provoke your children to anger." In other words, be careful not to annoy and irritate your child unduly. The word provoke means to be overly "rough." There are many things we can do to provoke children when disciplining them. Here are a few:

1. Perpetual fault finding
2. Excessive helicopter parenting
3. Setting unrealistic expectations
4. Playing favorites when disciplining
5. Inconsistency in applying discipline
6. Excessive punishment

Remember, the goal is honor and obedience. Honor means "to hold in high regard." And obedience means "to teach submission to authority." But the key to remember is that Paul teaches us that this should be done "in the Lord" and "of the Lord." Honor and obedience in the home should reflect the honor and obedience that God wants of all His children—including us fathers as God's children ourselves.

FIVE PRINCIPLES TO DISCIPLINE WISELY

ONE | SET BOUNDARIES

First, set clear limits for your child. Being disciplined for crossing a border that a child was not clear on is unfair to them. And your child is going to be hypersensitive to this unfair lack of clarity. Make sure your boundaries are communicated, clear, consistent, and not oppressive.

TWO | MATCH DISCIPLINE TO THE INFRACTION

Second, make sure when discipline is necessary it matches the extent of the offense. Nothing is more irritating to a child than the perception that their discipline is unbalanced. Kids have a keen sense of fairness, and if the punishment exceeds the impact of the infraction, they will fixate on the irrationality of the sentence, rather than the reason for the punishment.

THREE | MAKE IT AGE AND CHILD APPROPRIATE

Third, discipline should be age and child appropriate. If it's not, you run the risk of damaging their sense of dignity and souring their spirit. Even in discipline, you should respect and guard and even elevate their personhood. Since different kids have different wiring, you may also want to think through what discipline will be most meaningful to them.

FOUR | DELIVER IT WHEN CALM

Fourth, never hand out discipline in anger. If you are angry—and you may have the right to be—wait until the anger has subsided and you can discipline from a place of calm and sound judgment. And if you do error in these moments, do so on the side of grace and mercy. Anger will likely hijack your ability to be sound in judgment. The goal is not to communicate, "I love disciplining you," but rather "I love you, so I need to protect you from hurting yourself."

FIVE | KEEP THE GOAL IN MIND

Fifth, always keep the goal in mind. As Paul states in the text above, you are to bring your children up in the training and instruction of the Lord "that it may go well with you and that you may live long in the land." The end goal is to help them successfully navigate this period of dependence and become more interdependent on God in the future for a season that will be their own.

In the end, all parents have regrets about times when they disciplined poorly. By the time you are a grandparent, you'll have figured out something about parenting. Even so, in the present, you can minimize those regrets by helping your children and teaching them to respect authority and live within boundaries—while loving them all the way through a process that may be awkward for both of you.

REFLECTION & MENTORSHIP

BEGIN

- Understanding how to discipline a child requires a lot of wisdom and balance as a parent who is stewarding children toward interdependence on God.

UNPACK

- Would you characterize your parents more as harsh or lenient? Explain.
- How do you think this impacted your view of Father God?
- How does your upbringing impact how you discipline your children?

INFORM

- Looking back at your childhood, what about honor and obedience do you wish you would have learned from your parents?
- Of the five principles above, which do you need to give the most attention to?

LAND

- What is the biggest issue you need to address in your discipline and stewardship of your children?
- What steps do you need to take to address this issue?

DO

- With a friend or mentor, discuss the issue you need to address in your discipline.
- Additionally, share the steps you need to take to address the issue.
- Discuss this with your wife and children, along with the changes you would like to make.

RELATIONSHIPS ON THE MEND

"When a deep injury is done to us, we never heal until we forgive."

—Nelson Mandela

"Be kind to one another, tenderhearted, forgiving one another, as God in Christ forgave you."

—Ephesians 4:32

THERE IS PAIN IN EVERY FAMILY

None of us get through our childhood without some scars. It is not unusual to have many. Living in a fallen world and being raised by fallen parents, we are all impacted by our upbringing in both positive and negative ways. On the negative side, the scars often lead to disruption in relationships with parents and siblings. Many people dread uncomfortable family gatherings at Christmas, Easter, or Thanksgiving in which everyone pretends to be happy while struggling with unresolved issues.

When we marry, we bring into our own family any strained relationships we may have with our family members. This impacts our spouse and our children, who will quickly pick up on any dysfunctional or conflictual relationships within the larger family. Also, those damaged relationships continue to affect us and our emotional well-being, so any way you look at it, mending strained relations is worth the effort. Just as God is the ultimate reconciler, He has called us to the ministry of reconciliation; starting with our closest relationships makes perfect sense.

But how does one do that with a parent? With our fathers in particular? Usually, it starts with a conversation where you are willing to put on the table the issues that have caused you to keep your distance and guard your heart. Perhaps your father was an absentee dad, too busy at work to pay attention to you, or harsh and unfair in his discipline. Perhaps he abused drugs and alcohol, verbally abused your mother, or was unfaithful to her.

Reconciliation always begins with leaning into the truth. You are explaining to the one who has hurt you how you received that hurt and how it has impacted your life. Pretending that the pain does not exist doesn't work. Not speaking of it doesn't work. Only once you name the behaviors that hurt you and the impact that it had on your life will you start to find freedom. There is power in speaking the truth. Don't be surprised if emotions emerge as you share. Those emotions are often the unresolved pain that you have buried by not talking frankly about these issues.

Most fathers desire a relationship with their sons and didn't set out to hurt their kids. Your father may have simply raised you as he was raised. He may have been harsh and hurtful, but this behavior was what he knew, and he didn't rise above what he had experienced. In my experience, when confronted with a son's pain, fathers will often break, express sorrow, and even ask for forgiveness. Of course, there are also those who are narcissistic and so self-centered that they won't hear the truth of their children's experience, won't admit fault, and won't ask for forgiveness. But such men are an unusual exception.

Where forgiveness is sought, we have an opportunity to do as Paul admonishes: "Be kind to one another, tenderhearted, forgiving one another, as God in Christ forgave you" (Eph. 4:32). Forgiveness is a choice, and it emanates from kindness and compassion. Think of your dad listening to you share your hurt. He cannot change anything. He does not get a redo. He has wounded you, and he may feel terrible. Dads want a relationship with their sons as sons do with their dads. The only way through the wounds, hurt, and betrayal of what could have been is forgiveness. And you must forgive, forgive, and forgive again until our heavenly Father heals the wound.

Harder are those situations where forgiveness is not sought for and responsibility is not acknowledged. Here your choice is to forgive and let the hurt go or live in the ongoing pain and prison of your bitterness. It is hard to forgive, but living in the prison of bitterness is a worse alternative. The reality is that someone wounded you, a fact you had no control over. But to withhold forgiveness is to live in a prison of bitterness, and you can control whether you will make that choice.

The same principles can be applied to other family members with whom your relationship is strained. But what should happen after forgiveness? Forgiving another does not automatically mean that friendship will be quickly restored. Often, one needs to take baby steps toward a new kind of relationship based on truth and transparency. If it feels safe, you take another step, and if that feels safe, another step.

But there are also situations where a family member is toxic and their presence difficult. You do not have to live in bitterness, but you can and should set boundaries with poisonous family members so that your family (or you) are not impacted in hurtful ways. Boundaries can include specific behaviors that are off limits around you or your family, or you might forbid judgmental words that wound you still when you hear them again. Whatever these boundaries are, be accurate as to what is acceptable and what is not. Boundaries can also include how much time you allow a problematic family member to spend with you.

Fractured family relationships can often be repaired if you are willing to take the first step. Yes, forgiveness can be granted so that we don't live in a prison of our own making. And where necessary, boundaries can be established to ensure that relationships are kept in a safe and somewhat healthy zone in the future.

REFLECTION & MENTORSHIP
BEGIN
- Families are not perfect and sometimes require from us the courage to reconcile issues of the past so both parties can move on.

UNPACK
- What issues loom in your family of origin?
- What have you done, or not done, to address these issues?

INFORM
- Nelson Mandela makes a great point. When have you forgiven someone and found healing?
- How does knowing that Christ forgave you empower you to forgive others?

LAND

- What bitterness or pain have you left unaddressed that needs to be addressed?
- What steps do you need to take to work through this?

DO

- Share your need to forgive with a friend or mentor.
- Seek forgiveness from God for any bitterness or pain that looms in your past.
- Choose to let it go this week.
- Pray for strength and healing with a friend or mentor.

PREPARING FOR MARRIAGE

"Marriage is a school in which the pupil learns too late."
—*Author Unknown*

"Therefore a man shall leave his father and his mother and hold fast to his wife, and they shall become one flesh."
—*Genesis 2:24*

FALLING IN LOVE IS THE BEGINNING, NOT THE END

Between the day of the proposal and the wedding day, there's a tremendous opportunity for a man to prepare for a life together with his new bride. While a lot of time, energy, and money will be spent on the wedding event, marriage is much more than a single event in time; it is a lifetime of commitment that requires preparation. Many new husbands never take time for sober reflection on what their fiancé will be like—not only as a friend they love but a spouse they will live with. Life will be hectic during the engagement, and it will be tempting to spend most of it just trying to get to and beyond the wedding event. But as a man who will soon bear a new title, "husband," you need to plan for what's beyond the wedding. And for the next few weeks and months, you are given a unique opportunity to prepare for your upcoming marriage. The engagement period is a time to lay the foundation for what that life together will look like relationally, spiritually, emotionally, and physically. If you pay attention to these areas, you will launch your new marriage into a healthy future.

FOUR PREPARATION AREAS
ONE | RELATIONAL ONENESS

In the first blush of a love relationship, it is common for men to think exclusively about how much they have in common with their beloved and how similar the two of them are. It's almost predictable that shortly into the marriage you will be thinking, "Wow, we are different from one another. Now how do I negotiate with this woman?" Often, we are attracted to people who have different qualities than us only to discover after we are married that those very differences will make a relationship with each other challenging. In any marriage, understanding those differences and learning how to negotiate them is crucial.

Your engagement is a great time to observe your wife-to-be, discovering her moods, her pattern of navigating conflict, her highest values, her aspirations for the future, and the nuances of her personality that stem from her family of origin. You may want to reflect, journal, and discuss these observations with someone who has traveled the road ahead of you (and premarital counseling should facilitate this to some extent). The sooner you discover how to navigate these relational nuances effectively and how to address the inevitable conflict, the stronger your marriage will be. Remember, the goal is oneness, and in marriage, your commitment to relational unity is going to require effort. You cannot run from these issues in a lifelong commitment; you must run to them.

TWO | SPIRITUAL VITALITY

As a Christ follower, there are three people linked in marriage. You, your wife, and God. A spiritual connection is by far the most critical factor in a healthy, enduring, and happy marriage. And while most Christian couples assume this, living this out can be cumbersome. Many newlyweds soon discover that establishing spiritual connectedness through spiritual practices in the family means first discovering that two families of origin have different understandings about how this should look. Sometimes this will lead to conflict, which is counterproductive. But the best way to begin a marriage is to establish new spiritual traditions that are meaningful to you and your wife.

One non-negotiable should be taking the time to pray in person or by phone daily. Establishing simple spiritual practices like these are essential for spiritual oneness. Often, we overthink and overcomplicate spiritual connectedness.

But practices like daily prayer, spiritual discussion, weekly church attendance, and service together create valuable spiritual connections; these help develop further discussion and spiritual focus in marriage. These simple activities are spiritual and don't require a lot of you—just a little discipline. You need to take the initiative as the man, but also let your wife lead these efforts as well.

Another non-negotiable should be practicing biblical growth in your relationship. For example, texts like Ephesians 4:26—"Do not let the sun go down on your anger"—need to be committed to memory and practiced. This verse teaches a husband and wife that relational issues are a spiritual problem and should be addressed in a timely fashion. Developing a spiritual connection by being a husband of character is vital. While to this point you have been able to go home to "get away from people" and "let down," when you go home today your wife wants the best of you, not the worst of you. She is looking for a man and husband who is all in and lives out godly character in your relationship with her. You won't be able to hide from your new wife, so plan on your character being forged in a way you have never experienced. This is where marriage is hard, but it is a valuable tool in shaping a man—and a woman.

THREE | SEXUAL PURITY

When it comes to sex, God is explicit. Sex is an act is of such a high order that it is reserved for marriage, with one woman, wrapped in a lifelong commitment. How well you preserve and care for your sexual purity before marriage often determines how well you maintain your purity in your marriage. If you are willing to bend the rules and justify impurities during your engagement, what confidence does your spouse have that you will not justify other impurities inside of marriage? Fidelity begins well before marriage as we keep God's boundaries for the sexual relationship pure and undefiled; this sets a standard within marriage. Taking the lead here is challenging but not impossible. This not only includes the activity of sex but also how we keep ourselves pure from sexual perversions.

If you are engaged and sexually intimate with your fiancé, make a big decision and take godly action. Confess what is troubling your spirit, discuss your concerns with your fiancé, and make an agreement that you will stay pure from this moment until the wedding day. Your wife-to-be will respect you for it. More importantly, God will bless you for your obedience, and you will set a precedent for sexual wholeness, purity, and fidelity in your marriage.

FOUR | EMOTIONAL INTIMACY

One of the great definitions of intimacy is "into me you see." That is what emotional intimacy is. It's being willing to be fully transparent with your spouse about who you are, the struggles you have, and the issues you desire to overcome. In other words, emotional intimacy means that you hide no secrets from one another. Any decision you need to keep secret from your wife-to-be should not be a decision you make. Furthermore, these secrets have a way of coming out—destructively, not constructively.

Agree with your fiancé that neither of you will hide the truth of your life from the other. Be candid about your feelings, your emotions, your joys, and your struggles. Pray about them together. Don't enter into marriage with secrets but with a commitment to transparency, even when it's hard. Your marriage can survive transparency, but it may not be able to survive secrecy.

Engagement periods are times for preparation. Lay the foundation for your future life together. Don't waste this valuable time only preparing for a wedding—prepare for a new life together with the woman you love. You'll be glad you did.

REFLECTION & MENTORSHIP

BEGIN

- Engagement is a time to lay the foundation for what life together will look like relationally, spiritually, emotionally, and physically.

UNPACK

- 50% of all marriages, Christian or not, end in divorce. Why might this be so? How is this sobering?
- What is the story of your parents' marriage relationship? How do you think their example impacts you?

INFORM

- How is marriage a "school in which the pupil learns too late?"
- Genesis 2:24 commands that a man and woman are to "leave" and "hold fast." What does this mean?
- Where do you need to spend time preparing?

LAND

- What issue do you need to address in your relationship with your fiancé?
- What steps do you need to take to address this issue?

DO

- Create a plan of action based on the issues and challenges in the "Land" section above.
- Share the plan with a friend or mentor.
- Give your mentor permission to keep you accountable to the plan.

UNMARRIED AND LONGING TO BE

"People do not get married planning to divorce. Divorce is the result of a lack of preparation for marriage and the failure to learn the skills of working together as teammates in an intimate relationship."

—*Gary Chapman*

"House and wealth are inherited from fathers, but a prudent wife is from the Lord."

—*Proverbs 19:14*

MARRIAGE IS A WORTHY ASPIRATION

If you are single and want to be married, this is a noble aspiration. Aspiring to be married is a calling to become both a husband and a father. But it's also a longing for an ongoing relationship. Even Adam, the first man, wanted a relationship, and God saw it was good for him not to be alone—therefore God created woman. During your single years, you have an opportunity not only to develop the character that your wife may want in you, but to become the man God wants you to be. I know many married men who wish they had taken more time before marriage to prepare so that they might have handled the challenges of marriage with greater success. Even though marriage refines us as men, it is essential in your singleness not to miss the present opportunities for growth and change; these will increase your potential for a successful long-term commitment and relationship.

FOUR THINGS TO CONSIDER IN YOUR SINGLENESS
ONE | SELF-LEADERSHIP

All men need to learn self-leadership. Discovering the value of self-leadership as a single man is a great asset—and by the way, women like it. A man who cannot lead himself is destined for relational issues in other parts of life. Self-leadership is an intentional exercise. It touches many aspects of a man's life—timeliness, responsibility, conflict, self-care, grooming, building healthy relationships, avoiding unhealthy ones, and setting priorities. Self-leadership involves organizing our lives around priorities and values that lead to purposeful action rather than leaving each moment to happenstance. Here's a potential question that addresses this need and will drive you to prepare for marriage and family: "What are my relational priorities, and what's my plan for getting there?"

As a man, you must begin to determine your relational priorities now. Let's say you define your priorities broadly in this way:

1. A vibrant and growing relationship with God
2. Occupational fulfillment and impact in the world
3. Key friendships and relationships that make me a better man
4. A healthy and appropriate relationship with my family of origin
5. Mindset for ministry and contribution to things of eternal value
6. A healthy and committed marriage
7. God-fearing children

These are only broad examples, and you can borrow them if you like. But as a single man, naming your relational priorities in this way will allow you to begin devising a plan and determining the self-leadership needed for starting the journey. While at present you cannot do much about tending to a marriage or children, you can devise a plan for becoming a man that a wife and child would love and respect. And you can give a lot of attention at present to the first five priorities on the list above. You can devise a plan and focus on becoming the man God wants you to be. And by leading yourself in the present, you will be more prepared for leadership in marriage and of a family with children. But you must determine personal priorities first and then take a little time to reflect on how you are going to lead yourself there.

Having identified what's on your priority list, you now need to develop an intentional plan for getting there. This is where self-leadership moves from reflection into action. Perhaps there will be several small steps in each area where you can live out your personal priorities. Leaders are intentional, and your intentionality while you are single will serve you now—and if you get married, later. So start now by leading yourself.

TWO | DETERMINE YOUR VALUES AND GROW IN THEM

If you haven't taken the time to articulate your values, you need to. Doing so is a considerable step toward maturation, marriage, and stewarding your unique design. Many leaders declare business values and require employees to live by them but fail to declare personal values. Determining, stating, and living by your values is a vital step toward finding a woman who shares these values. Just take a few moments to reflect on this question:

> "What values do you want to guide your life, and how would you define those values?"

If you value honesty, for instance, what are the implications for living a life of honesty? And how does that value apply to your work, relationships, and even your relationship with God? Don't make the mistake of thinking of your values as static concepts. Instead, think of them as living principles that influence your actions, attitudes, and motives. You might state the value of honesty this way: "In all that I do, I will speak honestly, seek the truth, and do my best to live transparently with others." Here your value has become a guiding principle rather than a static idea written on a piece of paper. And as you look forward to marriage, you can aim to find someone who either shares or supports your value of honesty. And if a particular woman doesn't, then it might be a deal breaker.

THREE | DISCOVER YOUR IDENTITY IN SINGLENESS

Often, men and women get married because they are missing something in their lives and believe that a spouse will fill that void. While there is much to be said about a man and woman becoming "one flesh," many fail to remember that Jesus offers the relationship that completes us regardless of our married state. If you cannot come to a place of contentment and joy in your singleness, you will not find this in marriage; in fact, marriage might complicate your search. Your identity is not found in marriage, because marriage doesn't take the place of one's identity in Christ; it only compliments that identity. You are a complete person in Christ, married or not. Regardless of popular opinion, your spouse will not complete you; Jesus does.

FOUR | GET TO KNOW YOURSELF

Understanding yourself is a lifelong pursuit. So begin now. Get to know yourself well now because you will not be able to hide from your spouse. Here are some questions to consider:

How are you wired? What's your shadow side? What motivates you? What are the things that demotivate you? How do you recharge? At what times and in what circumstances are you most vulnerable to sin?

God made you unique, and as a man who lives in a sinful world, you have your vulnerabilities and tendencies. Knowing your weaknesses as you enter marriage is helpful. You will learn some lessons later, but willingly getting to know yourself now will benefit you, your future wife, and your marriage in the future.

It should be evident by now that there is plenty of self-leadership to do as a single man. Growing in these areas as an individual gives you time to focus on the very things that will be important when you become married. Furthermore, you will grow in your own personal emotional, spiritual, and relational health, which will give you the ability to influence others at a far deeper level than those who have not done this work in their own lives.

REFLECTION & MENTORSHIP
BEGIN

- Even though marriage refines us as men, it is essential in your singleness not to miss the present opportunities for growth and change that increase your potential for a successful long-term commitment and relationship.

UNPACK

- Why is singleness challenging?
- What is attractive to you about marriage?

INFORM

- Do you agree that divorce is a result of "lack of preparation?"
- Explain the proverb above in your own words.
- Of these four factors, which one presents your greatest challenge?

LAND

- What issues do you need to address as you learn more about your vulnerabilities?
- What steps do you need to take to gain a better sense of your own identity?

DO

- Take one action to prepare.
- Pray about this with a friend or mentor.

THIRTY VIRTUES THAT BUILD A MAN: A CONVERSATIONAL GUIDE FOR MENTORING ANY MAN

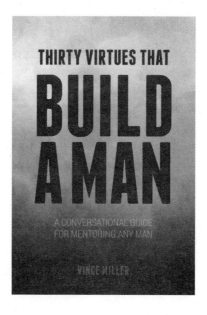

Men are a strategic force for change in the world, but they have an enemy, and it's not what you think. It's apathy. It is the appeal of inaction that lives within every man's heart.

Thirty easy-to-use lesson guides are perfect for men of all ages to use in private reflection or mentoring conversation with other men.

$10.99 paperback
96 pages
ISBN: 978-1-946453-31-0

https://beresolute.org/product/thirty-virtues-that-build-men/

20 LESSONS THAT BUILD A LEADER: A CONVERSATIONAL MENTORING GUIDE

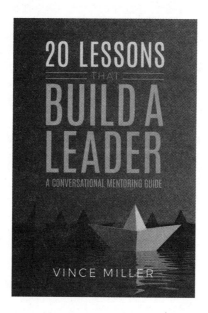

Mentorship is something many of us seek—but many of us feel unqualified to be a mentor of others.

This book includes 20 simple lessons that not only teach fundamental leadership lesson but empower a mentor with conversation that take the guesswork of mentoring other.

$10.99 paperback

96 pages

ISBN: 978-1-946453-63-1

https://beresolute.org/product/twenty-lessons-that-build-a-leader/

KEYNOTE SPEAKER TO MEN

Are you looking for a motivational and engaging communicator for your next men's retreat, conference, or event?

Engage men with a powerful message and inspire your men to action.

Like many young men, Vince Miller, born in the California, Bay Area, grew up without a father in the home. However, after his mother's second failed marriage, his grandfather took him in and mentored him into manhood. His compelling story of the problem and need for building better men has impassioned thousands of men to live with greater conviction and become the men God intended them to be. Prepare to be challenged with his message entitled, "Build Better Men."

To find out more or reach out to Vince Miller directly, go to our website.

www.beresolute.org/vince-miller